OXF[ORD]
PICTORIAL ENGLISH
DICTIONARY

Leisure and the Arts

THE
OXFORD – DUDEN
PICTORIAL ENGLISH
DICTIONARY

Leisure and the Arts

Oxford   New York

OXFORD UNIVERSITY PRESS

1986

Oxford University Press, Walton Street, Oxford OX2 6DP

Oxford New York Toronto
Delhi Bombay Calcutta Madras Karachi
Petaling Jaya Singapore Hong Kong Tokyo
Nairobi Dar es Salaam Cape Town
Melbourne Auckland

and associated companies in
Beirut Berlin Ibadan Nicosia

Oxford is a trade mark of Oxford University Press

The Oxford–Duden Pictorial English Dictionary first published 1981
First issued as a paperback 1984
This edition, under the title The Oxford–Duden Pictorial
English Dictionary: Leisure and the Arts, first issued 1986

Edited by John Pheby, Oxford, with the assistance of
Ronald Breitsprecher, Michael Clark, Judith Cunningham,
Derek Jordan, and Werner Scholze-Stubenrecht
Illustrations by Jochen Schmidt, Mannheim

British Library Cataloguing in Publication Data

The Oxford–Duden pictorial English dictionary.
—(Oxford paperback reference)
Leisure and the arts
1. Vocabulary—Pictorial works
428.1   PE1449
ISBN 0–19–281983–6

Printed in Hong Kong

Foreword

This pictorial dictionary is based on the Oxford–Duden Pictorial German-English Dictionary published in 1980. It was produced by the German Section of the Oxford University Press Dictionary Department in cooperation with the Dudenredaktion of the Bibliographisches Institut, Mannheim, and with the assistance of various British companies, institutions, and specialists. Numerous modifications of the text and illustrations of the original work have been carried out, especially regarding the depiction of everyday objects and situations, in order to allow greater scope for the treatment of these objects and situations in the context of English-speaking countries.

There are certain kinds of information which can be conveyed more readily and clearly by pictures than by definitions and explanations alone: an illustration will help the reader to visualize the object denoted by the word and to form an impression of the way in which objects function in their own technical field or in the everyday life of English-speaking countries. The layout of the illustrations and the text will be particularly useful to the learner. Each double page of the dictionary contains a list of the vocabulary of a subject together with a picture illustrating this vocabulary. This arrangement, and the presence of an alphabetical index, allows the book to be used in two ways: either as a key to the vocabulary of a subject or as an alphabetical dictionary in which the reader is referred to the section or sections in which the word is illustrated.

J.P.

Abbreviations

Am.	*American usage*
c.	*castrated (animal)*
coll.	*colloquial*
f.	*female (animal)*
form.	*formerly*
joc.	*jocular*
m.	*male (animal)*
poet.	*poetic*
sg.	*singular*
sim.	*similar*
y.	*young (animal)*

Contents

The arabic numerals are the numbers of the pictures

Community

THE
OXFORD–DUDEN
PICTORIAL ENGLISH
DICTIONARY

Leisure and the Arts

1 Musical Notation I

1-2 medieval (mediaeval) notes
1 plainsong notation (neumes, neums, pneumes, square notation)
2 mensural notation
3-7 musical note (note)
3 note head
4 note stem (note tail)
5 hook
6 stroke
7 dot indicating augmentation of note's value
8-11 clefs
8 treble clef (G-clef, violin clef)
9 bass clef (F-clef)
10 alto clef (C-clef)
11 tenor clef
12-19 note values
12 breve (brevis, *Am.* double-whole note)
13 semibreve (*Am.* whole note)
14 minim (*Am.* half note)
15 crotchet (*Am.* quarter note)
16 quaver (*Am.* eighth note)
17 semiquaver (*Am.* sixteenth note)
18 demisemiquaver (*Am.* thirty-second note)
19 hemidemisemiquaver (*Am.* sixty-fourth note)
20-27 rests
20 breve rest
21 semibreve rest (*Am.* whole rest)
22 minim rest (*Am.* half rest)
23 crotchet rest (*Am.* quarter rest)
24 quaver rest (*Am.* eighth rest)
25 semiquaver rest (*Am.* sixteenth rest)
26 demisemiquaver rest (*Am.* thirty-second rest)
27 hemidemisemiquaver rest (*Am.* sixty-fourth rest)
28-42 time (time signatures, measure, *Am.* meter)
28 two-eight time
29 two-four time
30 two-two time
31 four-eight time
32 four-four time (common time)
33 four-two time
34 six-eight time
35 six-four time
36 three-eight time
37 three-four time
38 three-two time
39 nine-eight time
40 nine-four time
41 five-four time
42 bar (bar line, measure line)
43-44 staff (stave)
43 line of the staff
44 space
45-49 scales
45 C major scale naturals: c, d, e, f, g, a, b, c
46 A minor scale [natural] naturals: a, b, c, d, e, f, g, a
47 A minor scale [harmonic]
48 A minor scale [melodic]
49 chromatic scale
50-54 accidentals (inflections, key signatures)
50-51 signs indicating the raising of a note
50 sharp (raising the note a semitone or half-step)
51 double sharp (raising the note a tone or full-step)
52-53 signs indicating the lowering of a note
52 flat (lowering the note a semitone or half-step)
53 double flat (lowering the note a tone or full-step)
54 natural
55-68 keys (major keys and the related minor keys having the same signature)
55 C major (A minor)
56 G major (E minor)
57 D major (B minor)
58 A major (F sharp minor)
59 E major (C minor)
60 B major (G sharp minor)
61 F sharp major (D sharp minor)
62 C major (A minor)
63 F major (D minor)
64 B flat major (G minor)
65 E flat major (C minor)
66 A flat major (F minor)
67 D flat major (B flat minor)
68 G flat major (E flat minor)

2 Musical Notation II

1-5 chord
1-4 triad
1 major triad
2 minor triad
3 diminished triad
4 augmented triad
5 chord of four notes, a chord of the seventh (seventh chord, dominant seventh chord)
6-13 intervals
6 unison (unison interval)
7 major second
8 major third
9 perfect fourth
10 perfect fifth
11 major sixth
12 major seventh
13 perfect octave
14-22 ornaments (graces, grace notes)
14 long appoggiatura
15 acciaccatura (short appoggiatura)
16 slide
17 trill (shake) without turn
18 trill (shake) with turn
19 upper mordent (inverted mordent, pralltriller)
20 lower mordent (mordent)
21 turn
22 arpeggio
23-26 other signs in musical notation
23 triplet; *corresponding groupings:* duplet (couplet), quadruplet, quintuplet, sextolet (sextuplet), septolet (septuplet, septimole)
24 tie (bind)
25 pause (pause sign)
26 repeat mark
27-41 expression marks (signs of relative intensity)
27 marcato (marcando, markiert, attack, strong accent)
28 presto (quick, fast)
29 portato (lourer, mezzo staccato, carried)
30 tenuto (held)
31 crescendo (increasing gradually in power)
32 decrescendo (diminuendo, decreasing or diminishing gradually in power)

33 legato (bound)
34 staccato (detached)
35 piano (soft)
36 pianissimo (very soft)
37 pianissimo piano (as soft as possible)
38 forte (loud)
39 fortissimo (very loud)
40 forte fortissimo (double fortissimo, as loud as possible)
41 forte piano (loud and immediately soft again)
42-50 divisions of the compass
42 subcontra octave (double contra octave)
43 contra octave
44 great octave
45 small octave
46 one-line octave
47 two-line octave
48 three-line octave
49 four-line octave
50 five-line octave

3 Musical Instruments I

1 lur, a bronze trumpet
2 panpipes (Pandean pipes, syrinx)
3 aulos, a double shawm
4 aulos pipe
5 phorbeia (peristomion, capistrum, mouth band)
6 crumhorn (crummhorn, cromorne, krumbhorn, krummhorn)
7 recorder (fipple flute)
8 bagpipe; *sim.:* musette
9 bag
10 chanter (melody pipe)
11 drone (drone pipe)
12 curved cornett (zink)
13 serpent
14 shawm (schalmeyes); *larger:* bombard (bombarde, pommer)
15 cythara (cithara); *sim. and smaller:* lyre
16 arm
17 bridge
18 sound box (resonating chamber, resonator)
19 plectrum, a plucking device
20 kit (pochette), a miniature violin
21 cittern (cithern, cither, cister, citole), a plucked instrument; *sim.:* pandora (bandora, bandore)
22 sound hole
23 viol (descant viol, treble viol), a viola da gamba; *larger:* tenor viol, bass viol (viola da gamba, gamba), violone (double bass viol)
24 viol bow
25 hurdy-gurdy (vielle à roue, symphonia, armonie, organistrum)
26 friction wheel
27 wheel cover (wheel guard)
28 keyboard (keys)
29 resonating body (resonator, sound box)
30 melody strings
31 drone strings (drones, bourdons)
32 dulcimer
33 rib (resonator wall)
34 beater for the Valasian dulcimer
35 hammer (stick) for the Appenzell dulcimer.

36 clavichord; *kinds:* fretted or unfretted clavichord
37 clavichord mechanism
38 key (key lever)
39 balance rail
40 guiding blade
41 guiding slot
42 resting rail
43 tangent
44 string
45 harpsichord (clavicembalo, cembalo), a wing-shaped stringed keyboard instrument; *sim.:* spinet (virginal)
46 upper keyboard (upper manual)
47 lower keyboard (lower manual)
48 harpsichord mechanism
49 key (key lever)
50 jack
51 slide (register)
52 tongue
53 quill plectrum
54 damper
55 string
56 portative organ, a portable organ; *larger:* positive organ (positive)
57 pipe (flue pipe)
58 bellows

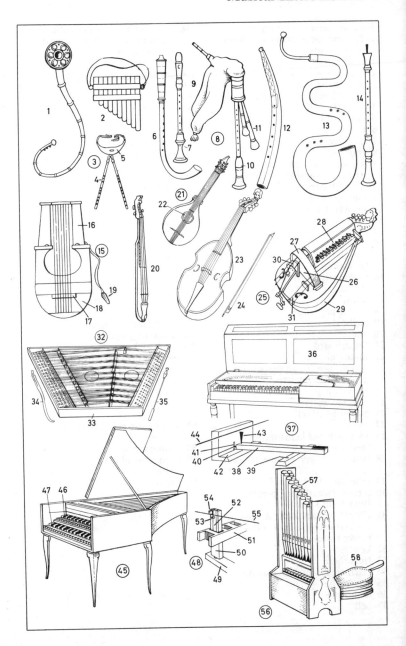

4 Musical Instruments II

1–62 orchestral instruments
1–27 stringed instruments, bowed
    instruments
1 violin
2 neck of the violin
3 resonating body (violin body,
    sound box of the violin)
4 rib (side wall)
5 violin bridge
6 F-hole, a sound hole
7 tailpiece
8 chin rest
9 strings (violin strings, fiddle
    strings): G-string, D-string, A-
    string, E-string
10 mute (sordino)
11 resin (rosin, colophony)
12 violin bow (bow)
13 nut (frog)
14 stick (bow stick)
15 hair of the violin bow
    (horsehair)
16 violoncello (cello), a member of
    the da gamba violin family
17 scroll
18 tuning peg (peg)
19 pegbox
20 nut
21 fingerboard
22 spike (tailpin)
23 double bass (contrabass, violone,
    double bass viol, *Am.* bass)
24 belly (top, soundboard)
25 rib (side wall)
26 purfling (inlay)
27 viola
28–38 woodwind instruments
    (woodwinds)
28 bassoon; *larger:* double bassoon
    (contrabassoon)
29 tube with double reed
30 piccolo (small flute, piccolo
    flute, flauto piccolo)
31 flute (German flute), a cross
    flute (transverse flute, side-
    blown flute)
32 key
33 fingerhole
34 clarinet; *larger:* bass clarinet
35 key (brille)
36 mouthpiece
37 bell

38 oboe (hautboy); *kinds:* oboe
    d'amore; tenor oboes: oboe da
    caccia, cor anglais; heckelphone
    (baritone oboe)
39–48 brass instruments (brass)
39 tenor horn
40 valve
41 French horn (horn, waldhorn), a
    valve horn
42 bell
43 trumpet; *larger:* B♭ cornet;
    smaller: cornet
44 bass tuba (tuba, bombardon);
    sim.: helicon (pellitone),
    contrabass tuba
45 thumb hold
46 trombone; *kinds:* alto trombone,
    tenor trombone, bass trombone
47 trombone slide (slide)
48 bell
49–59 percussion instruments
49 triangle
50 cymbals
51–59 membranophones
51 side drum (snare drum)
52 drum head (head, upper head,
    batter head, vellum)
53 tensioning screw
54 drumstick
55 bass drum (Turkish drum)
56 stick (padded stick)
57 kettledrum (timpano), a screw-
    tensioned drum; *sim.:* machine
    drum (mechanically tuned
    drum)
58 kettledrum skin (kettledrum
    vellum)
59 tuning screw
60 harp, a pedal harp
61 strings
62 pedal

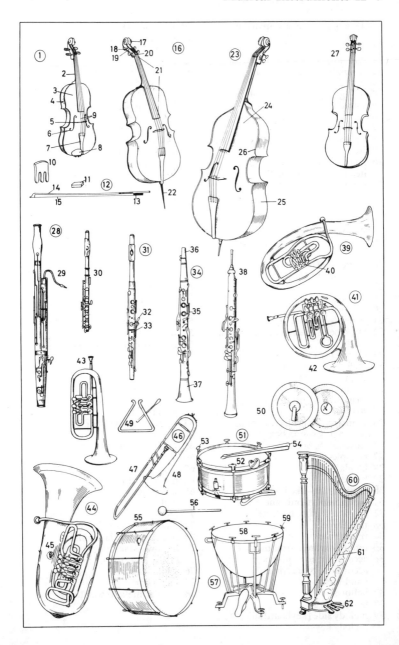

5 Musical Instruments III

1–46 popular musical instruments (folk instruments)

1–31 stringed instruments
1 lute; *larger:* theorbo, chitarrone
2 resonating body (resonator)
3 soundboard (belly, table)
4 string fastener (string holder)
5 sound hole (rose)
6 string, a gut (catgut) string
7 neck
8 fingerboard
9 fret
10 head (bent-back pegbox, swan-head pegbox, pegbox)
11 tuning peg (peg, lute pin)
12 guitar
13 string holder
14 string, a gut (catgut) or nylon string
15 resonating body (resonating chamber, resonator, sound box)
16 mandolin (mandoline)
17 sleeve protector (cuff protector)
18 neck
19 pegdisc
20 plectrum
21 zither (plucked zither)
22 pin block (wrest pin block, wrest plank)
23 tuning pin (wrest pin)
24 melody strings (fretted strings, stopped strings)
25 accompaniment strings (bass strings, unfretted strings, open strings)
26 semicircular projection of the resonating sound box (resonating body)
27 ring plectrum
28 balalaika
29 banjo
30 tambourine-like body
31 parchment membrane
32 ocarina, a globular flute
33 mouthpiece
34 fingerhole
35 mouth organ (harmonica)
36 accordion; *sim.:* piano accordion, concertina, bandoneon
37 bellows
38 bellows strap
39 melody side (keyboard side, melody keys)
40 keyboard (keys)
41 treble stop (treble coupler, treble register)
42 stop lever
43 bass side (accompaniment side, bass studs, bass press-studs, bass buttons)
44 bass stop (bass coupler, bass register)
45 tambourine
46 castanets

47–78 jazz band instruments (dance band instruments)

47–58 percussion instruments
47–54 drum kit (drum set, drums)
47 bass drum
48 small tom-tom
49 large tom-tom
50 high-hat cymbals (choke cymbals, Charleston cymbals, cup cymbals)
51 cymbal
52 cymbal stand (cymbal holder)
53 wire brush
54 pedal mechanism
55 conga drum (conga)
56 tension hoop
57 timbales
58 bongo drums (bongos)
59 maracas; *sim.:* shakers
60 guiro
61 xylophone; *form.:* straw fiddle; *sim.:* marimbaphone (steel marimba), tubaphone
62 wooden slab
63 resonating chamber (sound box)
64 beater
65 jazz trumpet
66 valve
67 finger hook
68 mute (sordino)
69 saxophone
70 bell
71 crook
72 mouthpiece
73 struck guitar (jazz guitar)
74 hollow to facilitate fingering
75 vibraphone (*Am.* vibraharp)
76 metal frame
77 metal bar
78 tubular metal resonator

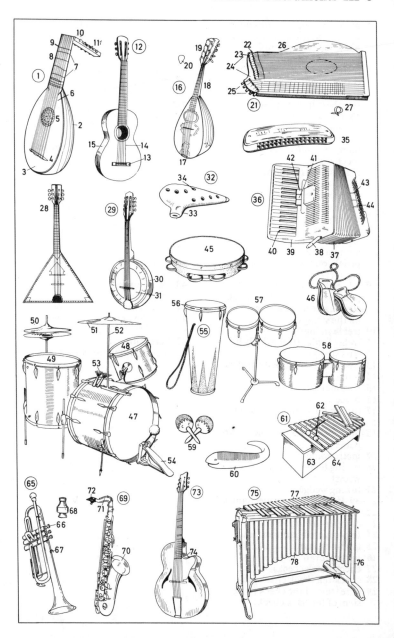

6 Musical Instruments IV

1 **piano** (pianoforte, upright piano, upright, vertical piano, spinet piano, console piano), a keyboard instrument (keyed instrument); *smaller forms:* cottage piano (pianino); *earlier form:* pantaleon, celesta, with steel bars instead of strings

2-18 piano action (piano mechanism)

2 iron frame

3 hammer; *collectively:* striking mechanism

4-5 keyboard (piano keys)

4 white key (ivory key)

5 black key (ebony key)

6 piano case

7 strings (piano strings)

8-9 piano pedals

8 right pedal (sustaining pedal, damper pedal; *loosely:* forte pedal, loud pedal) for raising the dampers

9 left pedal (soft pedal; *loosely:* piano pedal) for reducing the striking distance of the hammers on the strings

10 treble strings

11 treble bridge (treble belly bridge)

12 bass strings

13 bass bridge (bass belly bridge)

14 hitch pin

15 hammer rail

16 brace

17 tuning pin (wrest pin, tuning peg)

18 pin block (wrest pin block, wrest plank)

19 metronome

20 tuning hammer (tuning key, wrest)

21 tuning wedge

22-39 key action (key mechanism)

22 beam

23 damper–lifting lever

24 felt–covered hammer head

25 hammer shank

26 hammer rail

27 check (back check)

28 check felt (back check felt)

29 wire stem of the check (wire stem of the back check)

30 sticker (hopper, hammer jack, hammer lever)

31 button

32 action lever

33 pilot

34 pilot wire

35 tape wire

36 tape

37 damper (damper block)

38 damper lifter

39 damper rest rail

40 **grand piano** (horizontal piano, grand, concert grand); *smaller:* baby grand piano, boudoir piano; *sim.:* square piano, table piano

41 grand piano pedals; right pedal for raising the dampers; left pedal for softening the tone (shifting the keyboard so that only one string is struck 'una corda')

42 pedal bracket

43 **harmonium** (reed organ, melodium)

44 draw stop (stop, stop knob)

45 knee lever (knee swell, swell)

46 pedal (bellows pedal)

47 harmonium case

48 harmonium keyboard (manual)

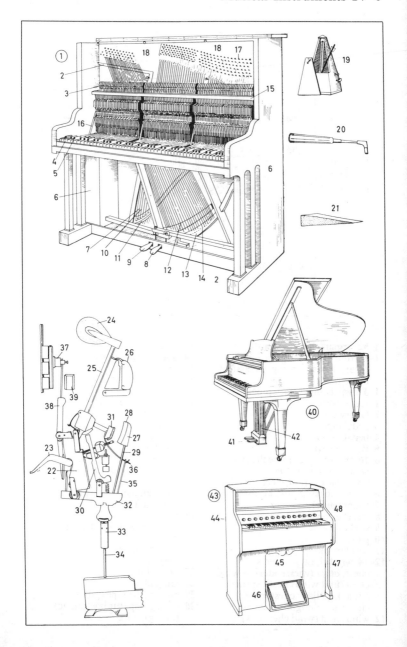

7 Musical Instruments V

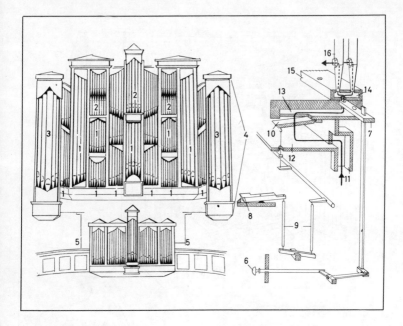

1–52 organ (church organ)
1–5 front view of organ (organ case) [built according to classical principles]
1–3 display pipes (face pipes)
1 Hauptwerk
2 Oberwerk
3 pedal pipes
4 pedal tower
5 Rückpositiv
6–16 tracker action (mechanical action); *other systems:* pneumatic action, electric action
6 draw stop (stop, stop knob)
7 slider (slide)
8 key (key lever)
9 sticker
10 pallet
11 wind trunk
12–14 wind chest, a slider wind chest; *other types:* sliderless wind chest (unit wind chest), spring chest, kegellade chest (cone chest), diaphragm chest
12 wind chest (wind chest box)

13 groove
14 upper board groove
15 upper board
16 pipe of a particular stop
17–35 organ pipes (pipes)
17–22 metal reed pipe (*set of pipes:* reed stop), a posaune stop
17 boot
18 shallot
19 tongue
20 block
21 tuning wire (tuning crook)
22 tube
23–30 open metal flue pipe, a salicional
23 foot
24 flue pipe windway (flue pipe duct)
25 mouth (cutup)
26 lower lip
27 upper lip
28 languid
29 body of the pipe (pipe)
30 tuning flap (tuning tongue), a tuning device

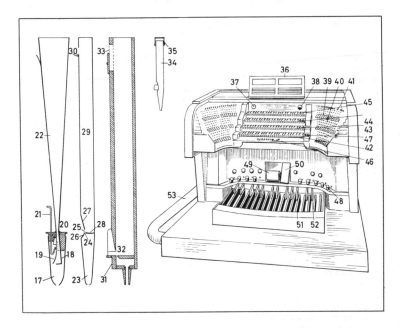

31-33 open wooden flue pipe (open wood), principal (diapason)
31 cap
32 ear
33 tuning hole (tuning slot), with slide
34 stopped flue pipe
35 stopper
36-52 organ console (console) of an electric action organ
36 music rest (music stand)
37 crescendo roller indicator
38 voltmeter
39 stop tab (rocker)
40 free combination stud (free combination knob)
41 cancel buttons for reeds, couplers etc.
42 manual I, for the Rückpositiv
43 manual II, for the Hauptwerk
44 manual III, for the Oberwerk
45 manual IV, for the Schwellwerk

46 thumb pistons controlling the manual stops (free or fixed combinations) and buttons for setting the combinations
47 switches for current to blower and action
48 toe piston, for the coupler
49 crescendo roller (general crescendo roller)
50 balanced swell pedal
51 pedal key [natural]
52 pedal key [sharp or flat]
53 cable (transmission cable)

8 Fabulous Creatures (Fabled Beings)

1–61 fabulous creatures (fabulous animals), mythical creatures
1 dragon
2 serpent's body
3 claws (claw)
4 bat's wing
5 fork-tongued mouth
6 forked tongue
7 unicorn [symbol of virginity]
8 spirally twisted horn
9 Phoenix
10 flames or ashes of resurrection
11 griffin (griffon, gryphon)
12 eagle's head
13 griffin's claws
14 lion's body
15 wing
16 chimera (chimaera), a monster
17 lion's head
18 goat's head
19 dragon's body
20 sphinx, a symbolic figure
21 human head
22 lion's body
23 mermaid (nix, nixie, water nixie, sea maid, sea maiden, naiad, water nymph, water elf, ocean nymph, sea nymph, river nymph); *sim.:* Nereids, Oceanids (sea divinities, sea deities, sea goddesses); *male:* nix (merman, seaman)
24 woman's trunk
25 fish's tail (dolphin's tail)
26 Pegasus (favourite, *Am.* favorite, steed of the Muses, winged horse); *sim.:* hippogryph
27 horse's body
28 wings
29 Cerberus (hellhound)
30 three-headed dog's body
31 serpent's tail
32 Lernaean (Lernean) Hydra
33 nine-headed serpent's body
34 basilisk (cockatrice)
35 cock's head
36 dragon's body
37 giant (titan)
38 rock
39 serpent's foot
40 triton, a merman (demigod of the sea)
41 conch shell trumpet
42 horse's hoof
43 fish's tail
44 hippocampus
45 horse's trunk
46 fish's tail
47 sea ox, a sea monster
48 monster's body
49 fish's tail
50 seven-headed dragon of St. John's Revelation (Revelations, Apocalypse)
51 wing
52 centaur (hippocentaur), half man and half beast
53 man's body with bow and arrow
54 horse's body
55 harpy, a winged monster
56 woman's head
57 bird's body
58 siren, a daemon
59 woman's body
60 wing
61 bird's claw

9 Prehistory

1-40 prehistoric finds

1-9 Old Stone Age (Palaeolithic, Paleolithic, period) and **Mesolithic period**

1 hand axe (*Am.* ax) (fist hatchet), a stone tool
2 head of throwing spear, made of bone
3 bone harpoon
4 head
5 harpoon thrower, made of reindeer antler
6 painted pebble
7 head of a wild horse, a carving
8 Stone Age idol, an ivory statuette
9 bison, a cave painting (rock painting) [cave art, cave painting]

10-20 New Stone Age (Neolithic period)

10 amphora [corded ware]
11 bowl [menhir group]
12 collared flask [Funnel-Beaker culture]
13 vessel with spiral pattern [spiral design pottery]
14 bell beaker [beaker pottery]
15 pile dwelling (lake dwelling, lacustrine dwelling)
16 dolmen (cromlech), a megalithic tomb (*coll.*: giant's tomb); *other kinds:* passage grave, gallery grave (long cist); *when covered with earth:* tumulus (barrow, mound)
17 stone cist, a contracted burial
18 menhir (standing stone), a monolith
19 boat axe (*Am.* ax), a stone battle axe
20 clay figurine (an idol)

21-40 Bronze Age and **Iron Age**; *epochs:* Hallstatt period, La Tène period

21 bronze spear head
22 hafted bronze dagger
23 socketed axe (*Am.* ax) with haft fastened to rings, a bronze axe
24 girdle clasp
25 necklace (lunula)
26 gold neck ring
27 violin-bow fibula (safety pin)
28 serpentine fibula; *other kinds:* boat fibula, arc fibula
29 bulb-head pin, a bronze pin
30 two-piece spiral fibula; *sim.:* disc (disk) fibula
31 hafted bronze knife
32 iron key
33 ploughshare (*Am.* plowshare)
34 sheet-bronze situla, a funerary vessel
35 pitcher [chip-carved pottery]
36 miniature ritual cart (miniature ritual chariot)
37 Celtic silver coin
38 face urn, a cinerary urn; *other kinds:* domestic urn, embossed urn
39 urn grave in stone chamber
40 urn with cylindrical neck

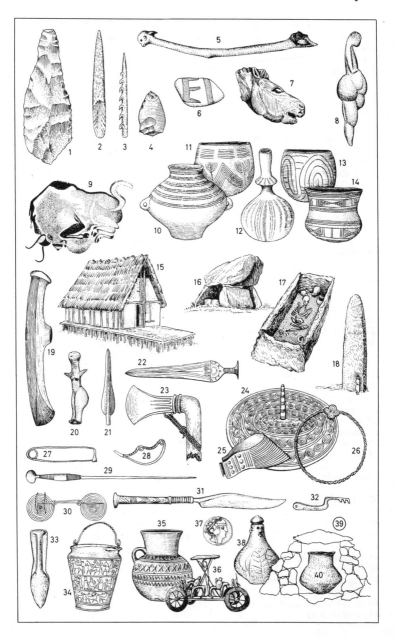

10 Chivalry

1 **knight's castle** (castle)
2 inner ward (inner bailey)
3 draw well
4 keep (donjon)
5 dungeon
6 battlements (crenellation)
7 merlon
8 tower platform
9 watchman
10 ladies' apartments (bowers)
11 dormer window (dormer)
12 balcony
13 storehouse (magazine)
14 angle tower
15 curtain wall (curtains, enclosure wall)
16 bastion
17 angle tower
18 crenel (embrasure)
19 inner wall
20 battlemented parapet
21 parapet (breastwork)
22 gatehouse
23 machicolation (machicoulis)
24 portcullis
25 drawbridge
26 buttress
27 offices and service rooms
28 turret
29 chapel
30 great hall
31 outer ward (outer bailey)
32 castle gate
33 moat (ditch)
34 approach
35 watchtower (turret)
36 palisade (pallisade, palisading)
37 moat (ditch, fosse)
38-65 knight's armour (*Am.* armor)
38 suit of armour (*Am.* armor)
39-42 helmet
39 skull
40 visor (vizor)
41 beaver
42 throat piece
43 gorget
44 epaulière
45 pallette (pauldron, besageur)
46 breastplate (cuirass)
47 brassard (rear brace and vambrace)
48 cubitière (coudière, couter)
49 tasse (tasset)

50 gauntlet
51 habergeon (haubergeon)
52 cuisse (cuish, cuissard, cuissart)
53 knee cap (knee piece, genouillère, poleyn)
54 jambeau (greave)
55 solleret (sabaton, sabbaton)
56 pavis (pavise, pavais)
57 buckler (round shield)
58 boss (umbo)
59 iron hat
60 morion
61 light casque
62 types of mail and armour (*Am.* armor)
63 mail (chain mail, chain armour, *Am.* armor)
64 scale armour (*Am.* armor)
65 plate armour (*Am.* armor)
66 **accolade** (dubbing, knighting)
67 liege lord, a knight
68 esquire
69 cup bearer
70 minstrel (minnesinger, troubadour)
71 **tournament** (tourney, joust, just, tilt)
72 crusader
73 Knight Templar
74 caparison (trappings)
75 herald (marshal at tournament)
76 tilting armour (*Am.* armor)
77 tilting helmet (jousting helmet)
78 panache (plume of feathers)
79 tilting target (tilting shield)
80 lance rest
81 tilting lance (lance)
82 vamplate
83-88 horse armour (*Am.* armor)
83 neck guard (neck piece)
84 chamfron (chaffron, chafron, chamfrain, chanfron)
85 poitrel
86 flanchard (flancard)
87 tournament saddle
88 rump piece (quarter piece)

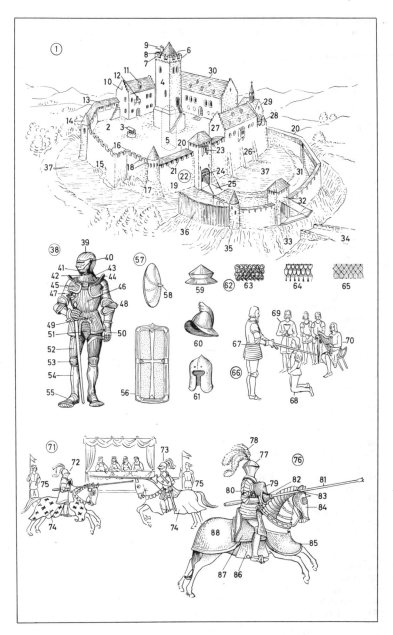

11 Church I

1–30 Protestant church
1 chancel
2 lectern
3 altar carpet
4 altar (communion table, Lord's table, holy table)
5 altar steps
6 altar cloth
7 altar candle
8 pyx (pix)
9 paten (patin, patine)
10 chalice (communion cup)
11 Bible (Holy Bible, Scriptures, Holy Scripture)
12 altar crucifix
13 altarpiece
14 church window
15 stained glass
16 wall candelabrum
17 vestry door (sacristy door)
18 pulpit steps
19 pulpit
20 antependium
21 canopy (soundboard, sounding board)
22 preacher (pastor, vicar, clergyman, rector) in his robes (vestments, canonicals)
23 pulpit balustrade
24 hymn board showing hymn numbers
25 gallery
26 verger (sexton, sacristan)
27 aisle
28 pew; *collectively:* pews (seating)
29 churchgoer (worshipper); *collectively:* congregation
30 hymn book

31–62 Roman Catholic church
31 altar steps
32 presbytery (choir, chancel, sacrarium, sanctuary)
33 altar
34 altar candles
35 altar cross
36 altar cloth
37 lectern
38 missal (mass book)
39 priest
40 server
41 sedilia
42 tabernacle
43 stele (stela)

44 paschal candle (Easter candle)
45 paschal candlestick (Easter candlestick)
46 sanctus bell
47 processional cross
48 altar decoration (foliage, flower arrangement)
49 sanctuary lamp
50 altarpiece, a picture of Christ
51 Madonna, statue of the Virgin Mary
52 pricket
53 votive candles
54 station of the Cross
55 offertory box
56 literature stand
57 literature (pamphlets, tracts)
58 verger (sexton, sacristan)
59 offertory bag
60 offering
61 man praying
62 prayer book

12 Church II

1 **church**
2 steeple
3 weathercock
4 weather vane (wind vane)
5 apex
6 church spire (spire)
7 church clock (tower clock)
8 belfry window
9 electrically operated bell
10 ridge cross
11 church roof
12 memorial chapel
13 vestry (sacristy), an annexe (annex)
14 memorial tablet (memorial plate, wall memorial, wall stone)
15 side entrance
16 church door (main door, portal)
17 churchgoer
18 graveyard wall (churchyard wall)
19 graveyard gate (churchyard gate, lichgate, lychgate)
20 vicarage (parsonage, rectory)
21–41 **graveyard** (churchyard, God's acre, *Am.* burying ground)
21 mortuary
22 grave digger
23 grave (tomb)
24 grave mound
25 cross
26 gravestone (headstone, tombstone)
27 family grave (family tomb)
28 graveyard chapel
29 child's grave
30 urn grave
31 urn
32 soldier's grave
33–41 funeral (burial)
33 mourners
34 grave
35 coffin (*Am.* casket)
36 spade
37 clergyman
38 the bereaved
39 widow's veil, a mourning veil
40 pallbearers
41 bier
42–50 **procession** (religious procession)
42 processional crucifix
43 cross bearer (crucifer)
44 processional banner, a church banner
45 acolyte
46 canopy bearer
47 priest
48 monstrance with the Blessed Sacrament (consecrated Host)
49 canopy (baldachin, baldaquin)
50 nuns
51 participants in the procession
52–58 **monastery**
52 cloister
53 monastery garden
54 monk, a Benedictine monk
55 habit (monk's habit)
56 cowl (hood)
57 tonsure
58 breviary
59 **catacomb**, an early Christian underground burial place
60 niche (tomb recess, arcosolium)
61 stone slab

13 Church III

1 Christian baptism (christening)
2 baptistery (baptistry)
3 Protestant clergyman
4 robes (vestments, canonicals)
5 bands
6 collar
7 child to be baptized (christened)
8 christening robe (christening dress)
9 christening shawl
10 font
11 font basin
12 baptismal water
13 godparents
14 church wedding (wedding ceremony, marriage ceremony)
15-16 bridal couple
15 bride
16 bridegroom (groom)
17 ring (wedding ring)
18 bride's bouquet (bridal bouquet)
19 bridal wreath
20 veil (bridal veil)
21 buttonhole
22 clergyman
23 witnesses [to the marriage]
24 bridesmaid
25 kneeler
26 Holy Communion
27 communicants
28 Host (wafer)
29 communion cup
30 rosary
31 paternoster
32 Ave Maria; *set of 10:* decade
33 crucifix
34-54 liturgical vessels (ecclesiastical vessels)
34 monstrance
35 Host (consecrated Host, Blessed Sacrament)
36 lunula (lunule)
37 rays
38 censer (thurible), for offering incense (for incensing)
39 thurible chain
40 thurible cover
41 thurible bowl
42 incense boat
43 incense spoon
44 cruet set
45 water cruet
46 wine cruet

47 holy water basin
48 ciborium containing the sacred wafers
49 chalice
50 dish for communion wafers
51 paten (patin, patine)
52 altar bells
53 pyx (pix)
54 aspergillum
55-72 forms of Christian crosses
55 Latin cross (cross of the Passion)
56 Greek cross
57 Russian cross
58 St. Peter's cross
59 St. Anthony's cross (tau cross)
60 St. Andrew's cross (saltire cross)
61 Y-cross
62 cross of Lorraine
63 ansate cross
64 patriarchal cross
65 cardinal's cross
66 Papal cross
67 Constantinian cross, a monogram of Christ (CHR)
68 crosslet
69 cross moline
70 cross of Jerusalem
71 cross botonnée (cross treflée)
72 fivefold cross (quintuple cross)

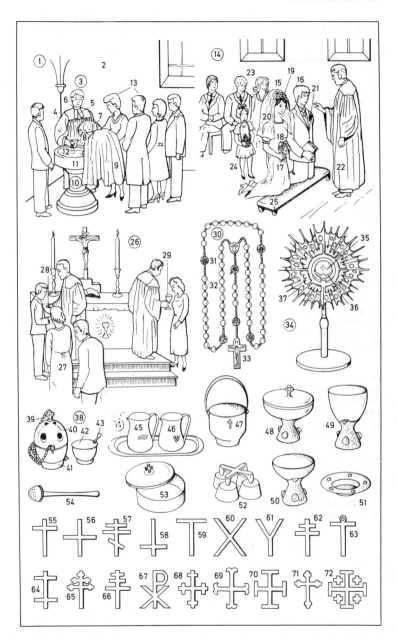

14 Art I

1–18 Egyptian art
1 pyramid, a royal tomb
2 king's chamber
3 queen's chamber
4 air passage
5 coffin chamber
6 pyramid site
7 funerary temple
8 valley temple
9 pylon, a monumental gateway
10 obelisks
11 Egyptian sphinx
12 winged sun disc (sun disk)
13 lotus column
14 knob–leaf capital (bud–shaped capital)
15 papyrus column
16 bell–shaped capital
17 palm column
18 ornamented column
19–20 Babylonian art
19 Babylonian frieze
20 glazed relief tile
21–28 art of the Persians
21 tower tomb
22 stepped pyramid
23 double bull column
24 projecting leaves
25 palm capital
26 volute (scroll)
27 shaft
28 double bull capital
29–36 art of the Assyrians
29 Sargon's Palace, palace buildings
30 city wall
31 castle wall
32 temple tower (ziggurat), a stepped (terraced) tower
33 outside staircase
34 main portal
35 portal relief
36 portal figure
37 art of Asia Minor
38 rock tomb

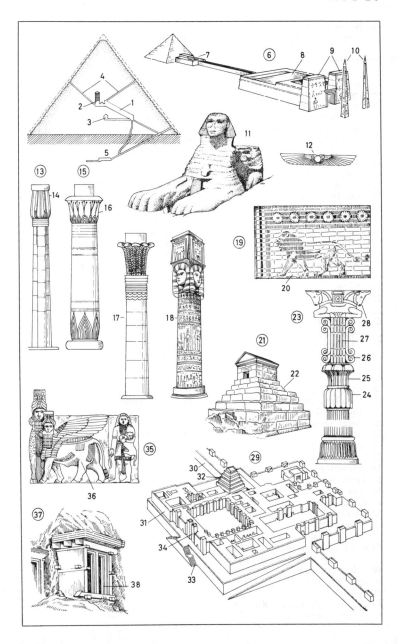

15 Art II

1–48 Greek art
1–7 the Acropolis
1 the Parthenon, a Doric temple
2 peristyle
3 pediment
4 crepidoma (stereobate)
5 statue
6 temple wall
7 propylaea
8 Doric column
9 Ionic column
10 Corinthian column
11–14 cornice
11 cyma
12 corona
13 mutule
14 dentils
15 triglyph
16 metope, a frieze decoration
17 regula
18 epistyle (architrave)
19 cyma (cymatium, kymation)
20–25 capital
20 abacus
21 echinus
22 hypotrachelium (gorgerin)
23 volute (scroll)
24 volute cushion
25 acanthus
26 column shaft
27 flutes (grooves, channels)
28–31 base
28 [upper] torus
29 trochilus (concave moulding, *Am.* molding)
30 [lower] torus
31 plinth
32 stylobate
33 stele (stela)
34 acroterion (acroterium, acroter)
35 herm (herma, hermes)
36 caryatid; *male:* Atlas
37 Greek vase
38–43 Greek ornamentation (Greek decoration, Greek decorative designs)
38 bead–and–dart moulding (*Am.* molding), an ornamental band
39 running dog (Vitruvian scroll)
40 leaf ornament
41 palmette
42 egg and dart (egg and tongue, egg and anchor) cyma

43 meander
44 Greek theatre (*Am.* theater)
45 scene
46 proscenium
47 orchestra
48 thymele (altar)
49–52 Etruscan art
49 Etruscan temple
50 portico
51 cella
52 entablature
53–60 Roman art
53 aqueduct
54 conduit (water channel)
55 centrally–planned building (centralized building)
56 portico
57 reglet
58 cupola
59 triumphal arch
60 attic
61–71 Early Christian art
61 basilica
62 nave
63 aisle
64 apse
65 campanile
66 atrium
67 colonnade
68 fountain
69 altar
70 clerestory (clearstory)
71 triumphal arch
72–75 Byzantine art
72–73 dome system
72 main dome
73 semidome
74 pendentive
75 eye, a lighting aperture

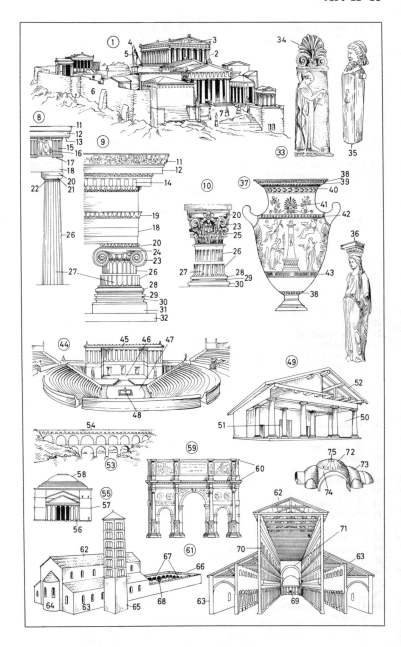

16 Art III

1–21 Romanesque art
1–13 Romanesque church, a cathedral
1 nave
2 aisle
3 transept
4 choir (chancel)
5 apse
6 central tower (*Am.* center tower)
7 pyramidal tower roof
8 arcading
9 frieze of round arcading
10 blind arcade (blind arcading)
11 lesene, a pilaster strip
12 circular window
13 side entrance
14–16 Romanesque ornamentation (Romanesque decoration, Romanesque decorative designs)
14 chequered (*Am.* checkered) pattern (chequered design)
15 imbrication (imbricated design)
16 chevron design
17 Romanesque system of vaulting
18 transverse arch
19 barrel vault (tunnel vault)
20 pillar
21 cushion capital
22–41 Gothic art
22 Gothic church [westwork, west end, west façade], a cathedral
23 rose window
24 church door (main door, portal), a recessed portal
25 archivolt
26 tympanum
27–35 Gothic structural system
27–28 buttresses
27 buttress
28 flying buttress
29 pinnacle
30 gargoyle
31–32 cross vault (groin vault)
31 ribs (cross ribs)
32 boss (pendant)
33 triforium
34 clustered pier (compound pier)
35 respond (engaged pillar)
36 pediment
37 finial
38 crocket
39–41 tracery window, a lancet window

39–40 tracery
39 quatrefoil
40 cinquefoil
41 mullions
42–54 Renaissance art
42 Renaissance church
43 projection, a projecting part of the building
44 drum
45 lantern
46 pilaster (engaged pillar)
47 Renaissance palace
48 cornice
49 pedimental window
50 pedimental window with round gable
51 rustication (rustic work)
52 string course
53 sarcophagus
54 festoon (garland)

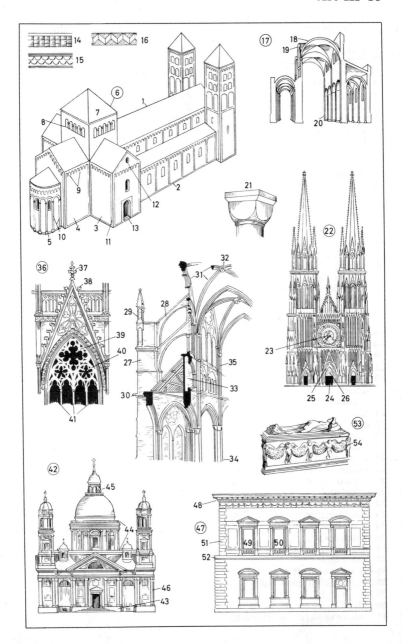

17 Art IV

1–8 Baroque art
1 Baroque church
2 bull's eye
3 bulbous cupola
4 dormer window (dormer)
5 curved gable
6 twin columns
7 cartouche
8 scrollwork
9–13 Rococo art
9 Rococo wall
10 coving, a hollow moulding (*Am.* molding)
11 framing
12 ornamental moulding (*Am.* molding)
13 rocaille, a Rococo ornament
14 table in Louis Seize style (Louis Seize table)
15 neoclassical building (building in neoclassical style), a gateway
16 Empire table (table in the Empire style)
17 Biedermeier sofa (sofa in the Biedermeier style)
18 Art Nouveau easy chair (easy chair in the Art Nouveau style)
19–37 types of arch
19 arch
20 abutment
21 impost
22 springer, a voussoir (wedge stone)
23 keystone
24 face
25 pier
26 extrados
27 round arch
28 segmental arch (basket handle)
29 parabolic arch
30 horseshoe arch
31 lancet arch
32 trefoil arch
33 shouldered arch
34 convex arch
35 tented arch
36 ogee arch (keel arch)
37 Tudor arch
38–50 types of vault
38 barrel vault (tunnel vault)
39 crown
40 side
41 cloister vault (cloistered vault)
42 groin vault (groined vault)
43 rib vault (ribbed vault)
44 stellar vault
45 net vault
46 fan vault
47 trough vault
48 trough
49 cavetto vault
50 cavetto

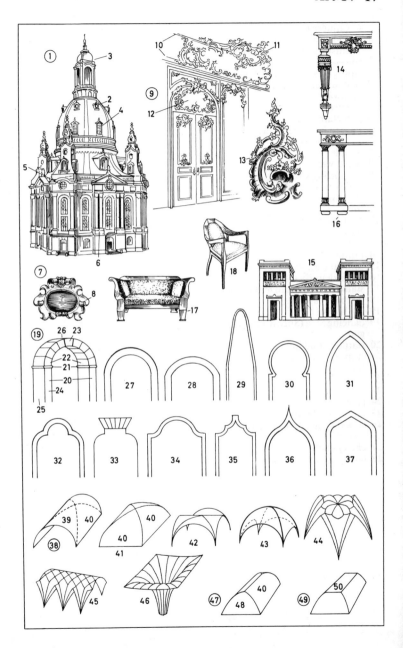

18 Art V

1–6 Chinese art
1 pagoda (multi–storey, multistory, pagoda), a temple tower
2 storey (story) roof (roof of storey)
3 pailou (pailoo), a memorial archway
4 archway
5 porcelain vase
6 incised lacquered work

7–11 Japanese art
7 temple
8 bell tower
9 supporting structure
10 bodhisattva (boddhisattva), a Buddhist saint
11 torii, a gateway

12–18 Islamic art
12 mosque
13 minaret, a prayer tower
14 mihrab
15 minbar (mimbar, pulpit)
16 mausoleum, a tomb
17 stalactite vault (stalactitic vault)
18 Arabian capital

19–28 Indian art
19 dancing Siva (Shiva), an Indian god
20 statue of Buddha
21 stupa (Indian pagoda), a mound (dome), a Buddhist shrine
22 umbrella
23 stone wall (*Am.* stone fence)
24 gate
25 temple buildings
26 shikara (sikar, sikhara, temple tower)
27 chaitya hall
28 chaitya, a small stupa

19 Artist's Studio

1–43 studio
1 studio skylight
2 painter, an artist
3 studio easel
4 chalk sketch, a rough draft
5 crayon (piece of chalk)
6–19 painting materials
6 flat brush
7 camel hair brush
8 round brush
9 priming brush
10 box of paints (paintbox)
11 tube of oil paint
12 varnish
13 thinner
14 palette knife
15 spatula
16 charcoal pencil (charcoal, piece of charcoal)
17 tempera (gouache)
18 watercolour (*Am.* watercolor)
19 pastel crayon
20 wedged stretcher (canvas stretcher)
21 canvas

22 piece of hardboard, with painting surface
23 wooden board
24 fibreboard (*Am.* fiberboard)
25 painting table
26 folding easel
27 still life group, a motif
28 palette
29 palette dipper
30 platform
31 lay figure (mannequin, manikin)
32 nude model (model, nude)
33 drapery
34 drawing easel
35 sketch pad
36 study in oils
37 mosaic (tessellation)
38 mosaic figure
39 tesserae
40 fresco (mural)
41 sgraffito
42 plaster
43 cartoon

1 sculptor
2 proportional dividers
3 calliper (caliper)
4 plaster model, a plaster cast
5 block of stone (stone block)
6 modeller (*Am.* modeler)
7 clay figure, a torso
8 roll of clay, a modelling (*Am.* modeling) substance
9 modelling (*Am.* modeling) stand
10 wooden modelling (*Am.* modeling) tool
11 wire modelling (*Am.* modeling) tool
12 beating wood
13 claw chisel (toothed chisel, tooth chisel)
14 flat chisel
15 point (punch)
16 iron-headed hammer
17 gouge (hollow chisel)
18 spoon chisel
19 wood chisel, a bevelled-edge chisel
20 V-shaped gouge

21 mallet
22 framework
23 baseboard
24 armature support (metal rod)
25 armature
26 wax model
27 block of wood
28 wood carver (wood sculptor)
29 sack of gypsum powder (gypsum)
30 clay box
31 modelling (*Am.* modeling) clay (clay)
32 statue, a sculpture
33 low relief (bas-relief)
34 modelling (*Am.* modeling) board
35 wire frame, wire netting
36 circular medallion (tondo)
37 mask
38 plaque

21 Graphic Art

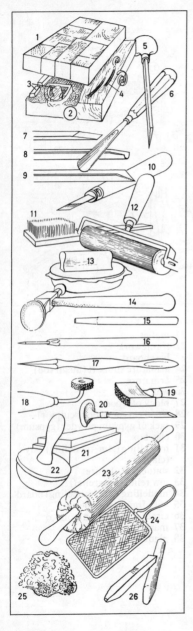

1-13 wood engraving (xylography), a relief printing method (a letterpress printing method)
1 end-grain block for wood engravings, a wooden block
2 wooden plank for woodcutting, a relief image carrier
3 positive cut
4 plank cut
5 burin (graver)
6 U-shaped gouge
7 scorper (scauper, scalper)
8 scoop
9 V-shaped gouge
10 contour knife
11 brush
12 roller (brayer)
13 pad (wiper)
14-24 copperplate engraving (chalcography), an intaglio process; *kinds:* etching, mezzotint, aquatint, crayon engraving
14 hammer
15 burin
16 etching needle (engraver)
17 scraper and burnisher
18 roulette
19 rocking tool (rocker)
20 round-headed graver, a graver (burin)
21 oilstone
22 dabber (inking ball, ink ball)
23 leather roller
24 sieve
25-26 lithography (stone lithography), a planographic printing method
25 sponge for moistening the lithographic stone
26 lithographic crayons (greasy chalk)
27-64 graphic art studio, a printing office (*Am.* printery)
27 broadside (broadsheet, single sheet)
28 full-colour (*Am.* full-color) print (colour print, chromolithograph)
29 platen press, a hand press
30 toggle
31 platen
32 type forme (*Am.* form)

33 feed mechanism
34 bar (devil's tail)
35 pressman
36 copperplate press
37 tympan
38 pressure regulator
39 star wheel
40 cylinder
41 bed
42 felt cloth
43 proof (pull)
44 copperplate engraver
45 lithographer (litho artist),
   grinding the stone
46 grinding disc (disk)
47 grain (granular texture)
48 pulverized glass
49 rubber solution
50 tongs
51 etching bath for etching
52 zinc plate
53 polished copperplate
54 cross hatch
55 etching ground
56 non-printing area

57 lithographic stone
58 register marks
59 printing surface (printing image
   carrier)
60 lithographic press
61 lever
62 scraper adjustment
63 scraper
64 bed

22 Script I

1-20 scripts of various peoples
1 ancient Egyptian hieroglyphics, a pictorial system of writing
2 Arabic
3 Armenian
4 Georgian
5 Chinese
6 Japanese
7 Hebrew (Hebraic)
8 cuneiform script
9 Devanagari, script employed in Sanskrit
10 Siamese
11 Tamil
12 Tibetan
13 Sinaitic script
14 Phoenician
15 Greek
16 Roman capitals
17 uncial (uncials, uncial script)
18 Carolingian (Carlovingian, Caroline) minuscule
19 runes
20 Russian
21-26 ancient writing implements
21 Indian steel stylus for writing on palm leaves
22 ancient Egyptian reed pen
23 writing cane
24 brush
25 Roman metal pen (stylus)
26 quill (quill pen)
27 Korean

1. 𓈖 [◎] 𓃟 𓏲

2. انصف بالشجاعة انا

3. Ⴆⴑⴐⴑⴜⴚⴖⴄ

4. განგე ჰონჯ

5. 圖書館
   图书馆

6. 新しい

7. וְיִדַּו וְאַרְאָה אֱרָאֵי יֵשֵׁב

8. 𒀭 𒈗 𒆠

9. वेउ चित्तमन्तरकाया प्रथिग-

10. ยัง ไร เกื้อน เก่า ลบ

11. உறிரண்ணியவர்மன்

12. རས་མ་ཐྲས་པ་སྟ་མིད་པ་

13. 𐤃 𐤏 𐤍 𐤋 𐤀 𐤆𐤆 𐤔𐤌

14. 𐎗 𐎌 𐎔 𐎚𐎚 𐎜 𐎂 𐎈𐎟

15. Τῆς παρελθούσης νυκτὸ

16. IMPCAESARI·

17. MINISUENIE

18. addiem feſtum

19. ᚠᚾᛈᛏᛁ:ᛁᛁ·ᛈᚾᛁᛏᛈᛈᛏᛏ·ᛈᛁᛏᛈᛏ·

20. Кожух генератора и

27. 책입니다

21.

22.

23.

24.

25.

26.

23 Script II

1–15 types (type faces)
1 Gothic type (German black-letter type)
2 Schwabacher type (German black-letter type)
3 Fraktur (German black-letter type)
4 Humanist (Mediaeval)
5 Transitional
6 Didone
7 Sanserif (Sanserif type, Grotesque)
8 Egyptian
9 typescript (typewriting)
10 English hand (English handwriting, English writing)
11 German hand (German handwriting, German writing)
12 Latin script
13 shorthand (shorthand writing, stenography)
14 phonetics (phonetic transcription)
15 Braille
16–29 punctuation marks (stops)
16 full stop (period, full point)
17 colon
18 comma
19 semicolon
20 question mark (interrogation point, interrogation mark)
21 exclamation mark (*Am.* exclamation point)
22 apostrophe
23 dash (em rule)
24 parentheses (round brackets)
25 square brackets
26 quotation mark (double quotation marks, paired quotation marks, inverted commas)
27 guillemet (French quotation mark)
28 hyphen
29 marks of omission (ellipsis)
30–35 accents and diacritical marks (diacritics)
30 acute accent (acute)
31 grave accent (grave)
32 circumflex accent (circumflex)
33 cedilla [under c]
34 diaeresis (*Am.* dieresis) [over e]
35 tilde [over n]

36 section mark
37–70 newspaper, a national daily newspaper
37 newspaper page
38 front page
39 newspaper heading
40 contents
41 price
42 date of publication
43 place of publication
44 headline
45 column
46 column heading
47 column rule
48 leading article (leader, editorial)
49 reference to related article
50 brief news item
51 political section
52 page heading
53 cartoon
54 report by newspaper's own correspondent
55 news agency's sign
56 advertisement (*coll.* ad)
57 sports section
58 press photo
59 caption
60 sports report
61 sports news item
62 home and overseas news section
63 news in brief (miscellaneous news)
64 television programmes (*Am.* programs)
65 weather report
66 weather chart (weather map)
67 arts section (feuilleton)
68 death notice
69 advertisements (classified advertising)
70 job advertisement, a vacancy (a situation offered)

Oxford 1
Oxford 2
Oxford 3
Oxford 4
Oxford 5
Oxford 6
Oxford 7
Oxford 8
Oxford 9
Oxford 10
Oxford 11
Oxford 12

13

'ɔksfəd 14

15

. 16
: 17
, 18
; 19
? 20
! 21
' 22
— 23
() 24
[] 25
,, `` 26
» « 27
- 28
... 29
é 30
è 31
ê 32
ç 33
ë 34
ñ 35
§ 36

24 Ethnology I

1 totem pole
2 totem, a carved and painted pictorial or symbolic representation
3 plains Indian
4 mustang, a prairie horse
5 lasso, a long throwing–rope with running noose
6 pipe of peace
7 wigwam (tepee, teepee)
8 tent pole
9 smoke flap
10 squaw, an Indian woman
11 Indian chief
12 headdress, an ornamental feather headdress
13 war paint
14 necklace of bear claws
15 scalp (cut from enemy's head), a trophy
16 tomahawk, a battle axe (*Am.* ax)
17 leggings
18 moccasin, a shoe of leather and bast
19 canoe of the forest Indians
20 Maya temple, a stepped pyramid
21 mummy
22 quipa (knotted threads, knotted code of the Incas)
23 Indio (Indian of Central and South America); *here:* highland Indian
24 poncho, a blanket with a head opening used as an armless cloak–like wrap
25 Indian of the tropical forest
26 blowpipe
27 quiver
28 dart
29 dart point
30 shrunken head, a trophy
31 bola (bolas), a throwing and entangling device
32 leather–covered stone or metal ball
33 pile dwelling
34 duk–duk dancer, a member of a duk–duk (men's secret society)
35 outrigger canoe (canoe with outrigger)
36 outrigger
37 Australian aborigine
38 loincloth of human hair
39 boomerang, a wooden missile
40 throwing stick (spear thrower) with spears

25 Ethnology II

1 Eskimo
2 sledge dog (sled dog), a husky
3 dog sledge (dog sled)
4 igloo, a dome-shaped snow hut
5 block of snow
6 entrance tunnel
7 blubber-oil lamp
8 wooden missile
9 lance
10 harpoon
11 skin float
12 kayak, a light one-man canoe
13 skin-covered wooden or bone frame
14 paddle
15 reindeer harness
16 reindeer
17 Ostyak (Ostiak)
18 passenger sledge
19 yurt (yurta), a dwelling tent of the western and central Asiatic nomads
20 felt covering
21 smoke outlet
22 Kirghiz
23 sheepskin cap
24 shaman
25 decorative fringe
26 frame drum
27 Tibetan
28 flintlock with bayonets
29 prayer wheel
30 felt boot
31 houseboat (sampan)
32 junk
33 mat sail
34 rickshaw (ricksha)
35 rickshaw coolie (cooly)
36 Chinese lantern
37 samurai
38 padded armour (*Am.* armor)
39 geisha
40 kimono
41 obi
42 fan
43 coolie (cooly)
44 kris (creese, crease), a Malayan dagger
45 snake charmer
46 turban
47 flute
48 dancing snake

26 Ethnology III

1 camel caravan
2 riding animal
3 pack animal
4 oasis
5 grove of palm trees
6 bedouin (beduin)
7 burnous
8 Masai warrior
9 headdress (hairdress)
10 shield
11 painted ox hide
12 long-bladed spear
13 negro
14 dance drum
15 throwing knife
16 wooden mask
17 figure of an ancestor
18 slit gong
19 drumstick
20 dugout, a boat hollowed out of a
   tree trunk
21 negro hut
22 negress
23 lip plug (labret)
24 grinding stone
25 Herero woman
26 leather cap
27 calabash (gourd)
28 beehive-shaped hut
29 bushman
30 earplug
31 loincloth
32 bow
33 knobkerry (knobkerrie), a club
   with round, knobbed end
34 bushman woman making a fire
   by twirling a stick
35 windbreak
36 Zulu in dance costume
37 dancing stick
38 bangle
39 ivory war horn
40 string of amulets and bones
41 pigmy
42 magic pipe for exorcising evil
   spirits
43 fetish

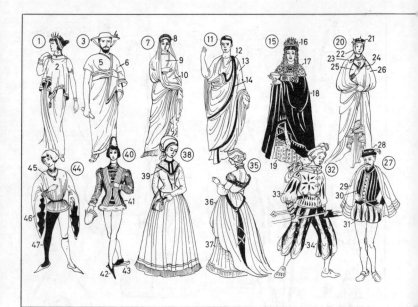

1 Greek woman
2 peplos
3 Greek
4 petasus (Thessalonian hat)
5 chiton, a linen gown worn as a basic garment
6 himation, woollen (*Am.* woolen) cloak
7 Roman woman
8 toupee wig (partial wig)
9 stola
10 palla, a coloured (*Am.* colored) wrap
11 Roman
12 tunica (tunic)
13 toga
14 purple border (purple band)
15 Byzantine empress
16 pearl diadem
17 jewels
18 purple cloak
19 long tunic
20 German princess [13th cent.]
21 crown (diadem)
22 chinband
23 tassel
24 cloak cord

25 girt–up gown (girt–up surcoat, girt–up tunic)
26 cloak
27 German dressed in the Spanish style [ca. 1575]
28 wide–brimmed cap
29 short cloak (Spanish cloak, short cape)
30 padded doublet (stuffed doublet, peasecod)
31 stuffed trunk–hose
32 lansquenet (German mercenary soldier) [ca. 1530]
33 slashed doublet (paned doublet)
34 Pluderhose (loose breeches, paned trunk–hose, slops)
35 woman of Basle [ca. 1525]
36 overgown (gown)
37 undergown (petticoat)
38 woman of Nuremberg [ca. 1500]
39 shoulder cape
40 Burgundian [15th cent.]
41 short doublet
42 piked shoes (peaked shoes, copped shoes, crackowes, poulaines)
43 pattens (clogs)

44 young nobleman [ca. 1400]
45 short, padded doublet (short, quilted doublet, jerkin)
46 dagged sleeves (petal-scalloped sleeves)
47 hose
48 Augsburg patrician lady [ca. 1575]
49 puffed sleeve
50 overgown (gown, open gown, sleeveless gown)
51 French lady [ca. 1600]
52 millstone ruff (cartwheel ruff, ruff)
53 corseted waist (wasp waist)
54 gentleman [ca. 1650]
55 wide-brimmed felt hat (cavalier hat)
56 falling collar (wide-falling collar) of linen
57 white lining
58 jack boots (bucket-top boots)
59 lady [ca. 1650]
60 full puffed sleeves (puffed sleeves)
61 gentleman [ca. 1700]
62 three-cornered hat

63 dress sword
64 lady [ca. 1700]
65 lace fontange (high headdress of lace)
66 lace-trimmed loose-hanging gown (loose-fitting housecoat, robe de chambre, negligée, contouche)
67 band of embroidery
68 lady [ca. 1880]
69 bustle
70 lady [ca. 1858]
71 poke bonnet
72 crinoline
73 gentleman of the Biedermeier period
74 high collar (choker collar)
75 embroidered waistcoat (vest)
76 frock coat
77 pigtail wig
78 ribbon (bow)
79 ladies in court dress [ca. 1780]
80 train
81 upswept Rococo coiffure
82 hair decoration
83 panniered overskirt

28 Infant Care and Layette

1 collapsible cot
2 bouncing cradle
3 baby bath
4 changing top
5 baby (new-born baby)
6 mother
7 hairbrush
8 comb
9 hand towel
10 toy duck
11 changing unit
12 teething ring
13 cream jar
14 box of baby powder
15 dummy
16 ball
17 sleeping bag
18 layette box
19 feeding bottle
20 teat
21 bottle warmer
22 rubber baby pants for disposable
   nappies (*Am.* diapers)
23 vest
24 leggings
25 baby's jacket
26 hood
27 baby's cup
28 baby's plate, a stay-warm plate
29 thermometer

30 bassinet, a wicker pram
31 set of bassinet covers
32 canopy
33 baby's high chair, a folding chair
34 pram (baby-carriage)[with windows]
35 folding hood
36 window
37 pushchair (*Am.* stroller)
38 foot-muff (*Am.* foot-bag)
39 play pen
40 floor of the play pen
41 building blocks (building bricks)
42 small child
43 bib
44 rattle (baby's rattle)
45 bootees
46 teddy bear
47 potty (baby's pot)
48 carrycot
49 window
50 handles

29 Children's Clothes

1–12 baby clothes
1 pram suit
2 hood
3 pram jacket (matinée coat)
4 pompon (bobble)
5 bootees
6 sleeveless vest
7 envelope-neck vest
8 wrapover vest
9 baby's jacket
10 rubber baby pants
11 playsuit
12 two-piece suit
13–30 infants' wear
13 child's sundress, a pinafore dress
14 frilled shoulder strap
15 shirred top
16 sun hat
17 one-piece jersey suit
18 front zip
19 catsuit (playsuit)
20 motif (appliqué)
21 romper
22 playsuit (romper suit)
23 coverall (sleeper and strampler)
24 dressing gown (bath robe)
25 children's shorts
26 braces (*Am.* suspenders)
27 children's T-shirt
28 jersey dress (knitted dress)
29 embroidery
30 children's ankle socks
31–47 school children's wear
31 raincoat (loden coat)
32 leather shorts (lederhosen)
33 staghorn button
34 braces (*Am.* suspenders)
35 flap
36 girl's dirndl
37 cross lacing
38 snow suit (quilted suit)
39 quilt stitching (quilting)
40 dungarees (bib and brace)
41 bib skirt (bib top pinafore)
42 tights
43 sweater (jumper)
44 pile jacket
45 leggings
46 girl's skirt
47 child's jumper
48–68 teenagers' clothes
48 girl's overblouse (overtop)
49 slacks
50 girl's skirt suit
51 jacket
52 skirt
53 knee-length socks
54 girl's coat
55 tie belt
56 girl's bag
57 woollen (*Am.* woolen) hat
58 girl's blouse
59 culottes
60 boy's trousers
61 boy's shirt
62 anorak
63 inset pockets
64 hood drawstring (drawstring)
65 knitted welt
66 parka coat (parka)
67 drawstring (draw cord)
68 patch pockets

30 Ladies' Wear II (Summer Wear)

1 mink jacket
2 cowl neck jumper
3 cowl collar
4 knitted overtop
5 turndown collar
6 turn-up (turnover) sleeve
7 polo neck jumper
8 pinafore dress
9 blouse with revers collar
10 shirt-waister dress, a button-through dress
11 belt
12 winter dress
13 piping
14 cuff
15 long sleeve
16 quilted waistcoat
17 quilt stitching (quilting)
18 leather trimming
19 winter slacks
20 striped polo jumper
21 boiler suit (dungarees, bib and brace)
22 patch pocket
23 front pocket
24 bib
25 wrapover dress (wrap-around dress)
26 shirt
27 peasant-style dress
28 floral braid
29 tunic (tunic top, tunic dress)
30 ribbed cuff
31 quilted design
32 pleated skirt
33 two-piece knitted dress
34 boat neck, a neckline
35 turn-up
36 kimono sleeve
37 knitted design
38 lumber-jacket
39 cable pattern
40 shirt-blouse
41 loop fastening
42 embroidery
43 stand-up collar
44 cossack trousers
45 two-piece combination (shirt top and long skirt)
46 tie (bow)
47 decorative facing
48 cuff slit
49 side slit
50 tabard
51 inverted pleat skirt
52 godet
53 evening gown
54 pleated bell sleeve
55 party blouse
56 party skirt
57 trouser suit (slack suit)
58 suede jacket
59 fur trimming
60 fur coat (*kinds:* Persian lamb, broadtail, mink, sable)
61 winter coat (cloth coat)
62 fur cuff (fur-trimmed cuff)
63 fur collar (fur-trimmed collar)
64 loden coat
65 cape
66 toggle fastenings
67 loden skirt
68 poncho-style coat
69 hood

31 Ladies' Wear II (Summer Wear)

1 skirt suit
2 jacket
3 skirt
4 inset pocket
5 decorative stitching
6 dress and jacket combination
7 piping
8 pinafore dress
9 summer dress
10 belt
11 two-piece dress
12 belt buckle
13 wrapover (wrap-around) skirt
14 pencil silhouette
15 shoulder buttons
16 batwing sleeve
17 overdress
18 kimono yoke
19 tie belt
20 summer coat
21 detachable hood
22 summer blouse
23 lapel
24 skirt
25 front pleat
26 dirndl (dirndl dress)
27 puffed sleeve
28 dirndl necklace
29 dirndl blouse
30 bodice
31 dirndl apron
32 lace trimming (lace), cotton lace
33 frilled apron
34 frill
35 smock overall
36 house frock (house dress)
37 poplin jacket
38 T-shirt
39 ladies' shorts
40 trouser turn-up
41 waistband
42 bomber jacket
43 stretch welt
44 Bermuda shorts
45 saddle stitching
46 frill collar
47 knot
48 culotte
49 twin set
50 cardigan
51 sweater
52 summer (lightweight) slacks
53 jumpsuit
54 turn-up
55 zip
56 patch pocket
57 scarf (neckerchief)
58 denim suit
59 denim waistcoat
60 jeans (denims)
61 overblouse
62 turned-up sleeve
63 stretch belt
64 halter top
65 knitted overtop
66 drawstring waist
67 short-sleeved jumper
68 V-neck (vee-neck)
69 turndown collar
70 knitted welt
71 shawl

32 Underwear, Nightwear

1-15 ladies' underwear (ladies' underclothes, lingerie)
1 brassière (bra)
2 pantie-girdle
3 pantie-corselette
4 longline brassière (longline bra)
5 stretch girdle
6 suspender
7 vest
8 pantie briefs
9 ladies' knee-high stocking
10 long-legged (long leg) panties
11 long pants
12 tights (pantie-hose)
13 slip
14 waist slip
15 bikini briefs
16-21 ladies' nightwear
16 nightdress (nightgown, nightie)
17 pyjamas (*Am.* pajamas)
18 pyjama top
19 pyjama trousers
20 housecoat
21 vest and shorts set [for leisure wear and as nightwear]
22-29 men's underwear (men's underclothes)
22 string vest
23 string briefs
24 front panel
25 sleeveless vest
26 briefs
27 trunks
28 short-sleeved vest
29 long johns
30 braces (*Am.* suspenders)
31 braces clip
32-34 men's socks
32 knee-length sock
33 elasticated top
34 long sock
35-37 men's nightwear
35 dressing gown
36 pyjamas (*Am.* pajamas)
37 nightshirt

38-47 men's shirts
38 casual shirt
39 belt
40 cravat
41 tie
42 knot
43 dress shirt
44 frill (frill front)
45 cuff
46 cuff link
47 bow-tie

33 Men's Wear

1–67 men's fashion
1 single–breasted suit, a men's suit
2 jacket
3 suit trousers
4 waistcoat (vest)
5 lapel
6 trouser leg with crease
7 dinner dress, an evening suit
8 silk lapel
9 breast pocket
10 dress handkerchief
11 bow–tie
12 side pocket
13 tailcoat (tails), evening dress
14 coat–tail
15 white waistcoat (vest)
16 white bow–tie
17 casual suit
18 pocket flap
19 front yoke
20 denim suit
21 denim jacket
22 jeans (denims)
23 waistband
24 beach suit
25 shorts
26 short–sleeved jacket
27 tracksuit
28 tracksuit top with zip
29 tracksuit bottoms
30 cardigan
31 knitted collar
32 men's short–sleeved pullover
   (men's short–sleeved sweater)
33 short–sleeved shirt
34 shirt button
35 turn–up
36 knitted shirt
37 casual shirt
38 patch pocket
39 casual jacket
40 knee–breeches
41 knee strap
42 knee–length sock
43 leather jacket
44 bib and brace overalls
45 adjustable braces (*Am.*
   suspenders)
46 front pocket
47 trouser pocket
48 fly
49 rule pocket
50 check shirt

51 men's pullover
52 heavy pullover
53 knitted waistcoat (vest)
54 blazer
55 jacket button
56 overall
57 trenchcoat
58 coat collar
59 coat belt
60 poplin coat
61 coat pocket
62 fly front
63 car coat
64 coat button
65 scarf
66 cloth coat
67 glove

34 Hairstyles and Beards

1–25 men's beards and hairstyles (haircuts)
1 long hair worn loose
2 allonge periwig (full-bottomed wig), a wig; *shorter and smoother:* bob wig, toupet
3 curls
4 bag wig (purse wig)
5 pigtail wig
6 queue (pigtail)
7 bow (ribbon)
8 handlebars (handlebar moustache, *Am.* mustache)
9 centre (*Am.* center) parting
10 goatee (goatee beard), chintuft
11 closely-cropped head of hair (crew cut)
12 whiskers
13 Vandyke beard (stiletto beard, bodkin beard), with waxed moustache (*Am.* mustache)
14 side parting
15 full beard (circular beard, round beard)
16 tile beard
17 shadow
18 head of curly hair
19 military moustache (*Am.* mustache) (English-style moustache)
20 partly bald head
21 bald patch
22 bald head
23 stubble beard (stubble, short beard bristles)
24 side-whiskers (sideboards, sideburns)
25 clean shave
26 Afro look (for men and women)
27–38 ladies' hairstyles (coiffures, women's and girls' hairstyles)
27 ponytail
28 swept-back hair (swept-up hair, pinned-up hair)
29 bun (chignon)
30 plaits (bunches)
31 chaplet hairstyle (Gretchen style)
32 chaplet (coiled plaits)
33 curled hair
34 shingle (shingled hair, bobbed hair)
35 pageboy style
36 fringe (*Am.* bangs)
37 earphones
38 earphone (coiled plait)

35 Headgear

1–21 ladies' hats and caps
1 milliner making a hat
2 hood
3 block
4 decorative pieces
5 sombrero
6 mohair hat with feathers
7 model hat with fancy appliqué
8 linen cap (jockey cap)
9 hat made of thick candlewick yarn
10 woollen (*Am.* woolen) hat (knitted hat)
11 mohair hat
12 cloche with feathers
13 large men's hat made of sisal with corded ribbon
14 trilby–style hat with fancy ribbon
15 soft felt hat
16 Panama hat with scarf
17 peaked mink cap
18 mink hat
19 fox hat with leather top
20 mink cap
21 slouch hat trimmed with flowers

22–40 men's hats and caps
22 trilby hat (trilby)
23 loden hat (Alpine hat)
24 felt hat with tassels (Tyrolean hat, Tyrolese hat)
25 corduroy cap
26 woollen (*Am.* woolen) hat
27 beret
28 bowler hat
29 peaked cap (yachting cap)
30 sou'wester (southwester)
31 fox cap with earflaps
32 leather cap with fur flaps
33 musquash cap
34 astrakhan cap, a real or imitation astrakhan cap
35 boater
36 (grey, *Am.* gray, or black) top hat made of silk taffeta; *collapsible:* crush hat (opera hat, claque)
37 sun hat (lightweight hat) made of cloth with small patch pocket
38 wide-brimmed hat

39 toboggan cap (skiing cap, ski cap)
40 workman's cap

36 Jewellery (*Am.* Jewelry)

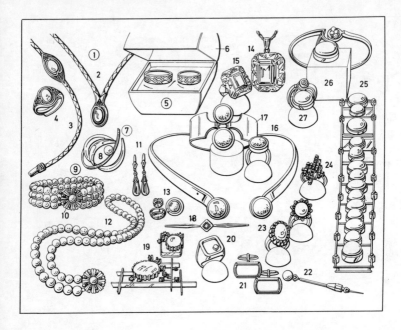

1 set of jewellery (*Am.* jewelry)
2 necklace
3 bracelet
4 ring
5 wedding rings
6 wedding ring box
7 brooch, a pearl brooch
8 pearl
9 cultured pearl bracelet
10 clasp, a white gold clasp
11 pendant earrings (drop earrings)
12 cultured pearl necklace
13 earrings
14 gemstone pendant
15 gemstone ring
16 choker (collar, neckband)
17 bangle
18 diamond pin
19 modern-style brooches
20 man's ring
21 cuff links
22 tiepin
23 diamond ring with pearl
24 modern-style diamond ring
25 gemstone bracelet

26 asymmetrical bangle
27 asymmetrical ring
28 ivory necklace
29 ivory rose
30 ivory brooch
31 jewel box (jewel case)
32 pearl necklace
33 bracelet watch
34 coral necklace
35 charms
36 coin bracelet
37 gold coin
38 coin setting
39 link
40 signet ring
41 engraving (monogram)
42–86 cuts and forms

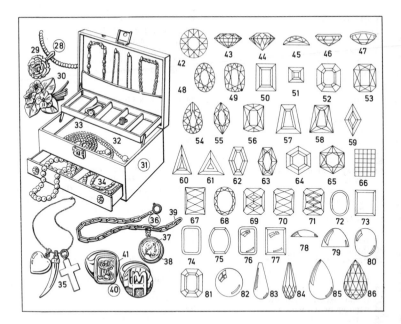

42–71 faceted stones
42–43 standard round cut
44 brilliant cut
45 rose cut
46 flat table
47 table en cabochon
48 standard cut
49 standard antique cut
50 rectangular step-cut
51 square step-cut
52 octagonal step-cut
53 octagonal cross-cut
54 standard pear-shape (pendeloque)
55 marquise (navette)
56 standard barrel-shape
57 trapezium step-cut
58 trapezium cross-cut
59 rhombus step-cut
60–61 triangular step-cut
62 hexagonal step-cut
63 oval hexagonal cross-cut
64 round hexagonal step-cut
65 round hexagonal cross-cut
66 chequer-board cut

67 triangle cut
68–71 fancy cuts
72–77 ring gemstones
72 oval flat table
73 rectangular flat table
74 octagonal flat table
75 barrel-shape
76 antique table en cabochon
77 rectangular table en cabochon
78–81 cabochons
78 round cabochon (simple cabochon)
79 high dome (high cabochon)
80 oval cabochon
81 octagonal cabochon
82–86 spheres and pear-shapes
82 plain sphere
83 plain pear-shape
84 faceted pear-shape
85 plain drop
86 faceted briolette

37 Types of Dwelling

1-53 detached house
1 basement
2 ground floor (*Am.* first floor)
3 upper floor (first floor, *Am.* second floor)
4 loft
5 roof, a gable roof (saddle roof, saddleback roof)
6 gutter
7 ridge
8 verge with bargeboards
9 eaves, rafter-supported eaves
10 chimney
11 gutter
12 swan's neck (swan-neck)
13 rainwater pipe (downpipe, *Am.* downspout, leader)
14 vertical pipe, a cast-iron pipe
15 gable (gable end)
16 glass wall
17 base course (plinth)
18 balcony
19 parapet
20 flower box
21 French window (French windows) opening on to the balcony
22 double casement window
23 single casement window
24 window breast with window sill
25 lintel (window head)
26 reveal
27 cellar window (basement window)
28 rolling shutter
29 rolling shutter frame
30 window shutter (folding shutter)
31 shutter catch
32 garage with tool shed
33 espalier
34 batten door (ledged door)
35 fanlight with mullion and transom
36 terrace
37 garden wall with coping stones
38 garden light
39 steps
40 rockery (rock garden)
41 outside tap (*Am.* faucet) for the hose
42 garden hose
43 lawn sprinkler
44 paddling pool
45 stepping stones
46 sunbathing area (lawn)
47 deck-chair
48 sunshade (garden parasol)
49 garden chair
50 garden table
51 frame for beating carpets
52 garage driveway

53 fence, a wooden fence
54-57 housing estate (housing development)
54 house on a housing estate (on a housing development)
55 pent roof (penthouse roof)
56 dormer (dormer window)
57 garden
58-63 terraced house [one of a row of terraced houses], **stepped**
58 front garden
59 hedge
60 pavement (*Am.* sidewalk, walkway)
61 street (road)
62 street lamp (street light)
63 litter bin (*Am.* litter basket)
64-68 house divided into two flats (*Am.* house divided into two apartments, duplex house)
64 hip (hipped) roof
65 front door
66 front steps
67 canopy
68 flower window (window for house plants)
69-71 pair of semi-detached houses divided into flour flats (*Am.* apartments)
69 balcony
70 sun lounge (*Am.* sun parlor)
71 awning (sun blind, sunshade)
72-76 block of flats (*Am.* apartment building, apartment house) with access balconies
72 staircase
73 balcony
74 studio flat (*Am.* studio apartment)
75 sun roof, a sun terrace
76 open space
77-81 multi-storey block of flats (*Am.* multistory apartment building, multistory apartment house)
77 flat roof
78 pent roof (shed roof, lean-to roof)
79 garage
80 pergola
81 staircase window
82 high-rise block of flats (*Am.* high-rise apartment building, high-rise apartment house)
83 penthouse
84-86 weekend house, a timber house
84 horizontal boarding
85 natural stone base course (natural stone plinth)
86 strip windows (ribbon windows)

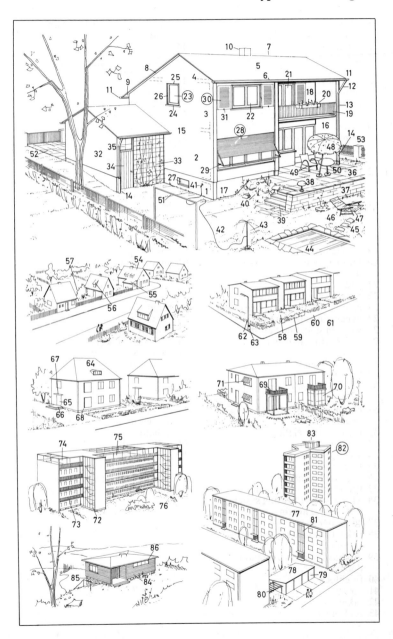

38 Roof and Boiler Room

1-29 attic
1 roof cladding (roof covering)
2 skylight
3 gangway
4 cat ladder (roof ladder)
5 chimney
6 roof hook
7 dormer window (dormer)
8 snow guard (roof guard)
9 gutter
10 rainwater pipe (downpipe, *Am.* downspout, leader)
11 eaves
12 pitched roof
13 trapdoor
14 hatch
15 ladder
16 stile
17 rung
18 loft (attic)
19 wooden partition
20 lumber room door (boxroom door)
21 padlock
22 hook [for washing line]
23 clothes line (washing line)
24 expansion tank for boiler
25 wooden steps and balustrade
26 string (*Am.* stringer)
27 step
28 handrail (guard rail)
29 baluster
30 lightning conductor (lightning rod)
31 **chimney sweep** (*Am.* chimney sweeper)
32 brush with weight
33 shoulder iron
34 sack for soot
35 flue brush
36 broom (besom)
37 broomstick (broom handle)
38-81 hot-water heating system, full central heating
38-43 boiler room
38 coke-fired central heating system
39 ash box door (*Am.* cleanout door)
40 flueblock
41 poker
42 rake
43 coal shovel

44-60 oil-fired central heating system
44 oil tank
45 manhole
46 manhole cover
47 tank inlet
48 dome cover
49 tank bottom valve
50 fuel oil (heating oil)
51 air-bleed duct
52 air vent cap
53 oil level pipe
54 oil gauge (*Am.* gage)
55 suction pipe
56 return pipe
57 central heating furnace (oil heating furnace)
58-60 oil burner
58 fan
59 electric motor
60 covered pilot light
61 charging door
62 inspection window
63 water gauge (*Am.* gage)
64 furnace thermometer
65 bleeder
66 furnace bed
67 control panel
68 hot water tank (boiler)
69 overflow pipe (overflow)
70 safety valve
71 main distribution pipe
72 lagging
73 valve
74 flow pipe
75 regulating valve
76 radiator
77 radiator rib
78 room thermostat
79 return pipe (return)
80 return pipe [in two-pipe system]
81 smoke outlet (smoke extract)

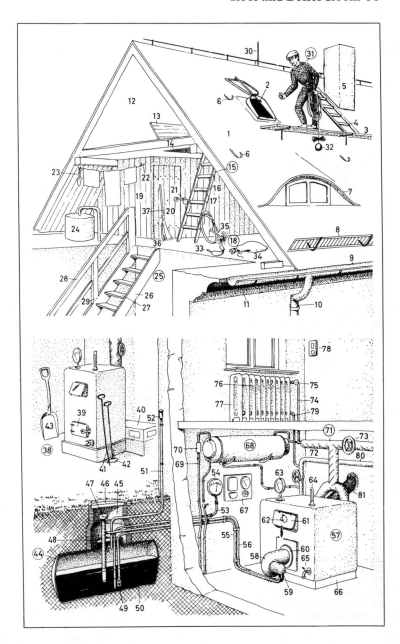

1 housewife
2 refrigerator (fridge, *Am.* icebox)
3 refrigerator shelf
4 salad drawer
5 frozen food compartment
6 bottle rack (in storage door)
7 upright freezer
8 wall cupboard, a kitchen
  cupboard
9 base unit
10 cutlery drawer
11 working top
12–17 cooker unit
12 electric cooker (*also:* gas cooker)
13 oven
14 oven window
15 hotplate (automatic high–speed
   plate)
16 kettle (whistling kettle)
17 cooker hood
18 pot holder
19 pot holder rack
20 kitchen clock
21 timer
22 hand mixer
23 whisk
24 electric coffee grinder (with
   rotating blades)

25 lead
26 wall socket
27 corner unit
28 revolving shelf
29 pot (cooking pot)
30 jug
31 spice rack
32 spice jar
33–36 sink unit
33 dish drainer
34 tea plate
35 sink
36 water tap (*Am.* faucet) (mixer
   tap, *Am.* mixing faucet)
37 pot plant, a foliage plant
38 coffee maker
39 kitchen lamp
40 dishwasher (dishwashing
   machine)
41 dish rack
42 dinner plate
43 kitchen chair
44 kitchen table

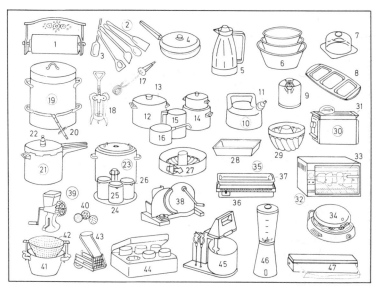

1 general–purpose roll holder with kitchen roll (paper towels)
2 set of wooden spoons
3 mixing spoon
4 frying pan
5 Thermos jug
6 set of bowls
7 cheese dish with glass cover
8 three–compartment dish
9 lemon squeezer
10 whistling kettle
11 whistle
12–16 pan set
12 pot (cooking pot)
13 lid
14 casserole dish
15 milk pot
16 saucepan
17 immersion heater
18 corkscrew [with levers]
19 juice extractor
20 tube clamp (tube clip)
21 pressure cooker
22 pressure valve
23 fruit preserver
24 removable rack
25 preserving jar
26 rubber ring

27 spring form
28 cake tin
29 cake tin
30 toaster
31 rack for rolls
32 rotisserie
33 spit
34 electric waffle iron
35 sliding–weight scales
36 sliding weight
37 scale pan
38 food slicer
39 mincer (*Am.* meat chopper)
40 blades
41 chip pan
42 basket
43 potato chipper
44 yoghurt maker
45 mixer
46 blender
47 bag sealer

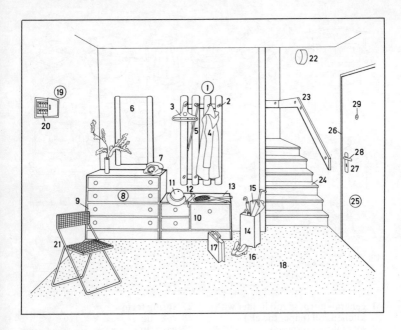

1–29 hall (entrance hall)
1 coat rack
2 coat hook
3 coat hanger
4 rain cape
5 walking stick
6 hall mirror
7 telephone
8 chest of drawers for shoes, etc.
9 drawer
10 seat
11 ladies' hat
12 telescopic umbrella
13 tennis rackets (tennis racquets)
14 umbrella stand
15 umbrella
16 shoes
17 briefcase
18 fitted carpet
19 fuse box
20 miniature circuit breaker
21 tubular steel chair
22 stair light
23 handrail
24 step

25 front door
26 door frame
27 door lock
28 door handle
29 spyhole

1 wall units	23 seat cushion (cushion)
2 side wall	24 settee
3 bookshelf	25 back cushion
4 row of books	26 [round] corner section
5 display cabinet unit	27 scatter cushion
6 cupboard base unit	28 coffee table
7 cupboard unit	29 ashtray
8 television set (TV set)	30 tray
9 stereo system (stereo equipment)	31 whisky (whiskey) bottle
10 speaker (loudspeaker)	32 soda water bottle (soda bottle)
11 pipe rack	**33–34 dining set**
12 pipe	33 dining table
13 globe	34 chair
14 brass kettle	35 net curtain
15 telescope	36 indoor plants (houseplants)
16 mantle clock	
17 bust	
18 encyclopaedia [in several volumes]	
19 room divider	
20 drinks cupboard	
21–26 upholstered suite (seating group)	
21 armchair	
22 arm	

1 wardrobe (*Am.* clothes closet)
2 linen shelf
3 cane chair
4–13 double bed (*sim.:* double divan)
4–6 bedstead
4 foot of the bed
5 bed frame
6 headboard
7 bedspread
8 duvet, a quilted duvet
9 sheet, a linen sheet
10 mattress, a foam mattress with drill tick
11 [wedge-shaped] bolster
12–13 pillow
12 pillowcase (pillowslip)
13 tick
14 bookshelf [attached to the headboard]
15 reading lamp
16 electric alarm clock
17 bedside cabinet
18 drawer
19 bedroom lamp

20 picture
21 picture frame
22 bedside rug
23 fitted carpet
24 dressing stool
25 dressing table
26 perfume spray
27 perfume bottle
28 powder box
29 dressing-table mirror (mirror)

1-11 dining set
1 dining table
2 table leg
3 table top
4 place mat
5 place (place setting, cover)
6 soup plate (deep plate)
7 dinner plate
8 soup tureen
9 wineglass
10 dining chair
11 seat
12 lamp (pendant lamp)
13 curtains
14 net curtain
15 curtain rail
16 carpet
17 wall unit
18 glass door
19 shelf
20 sideboard
21 cutlery drawer
22 linen drawer
23 base
24 round tray

25 pot plant
26 china cabinet (display cabinet)
27 coffee set (coffee service)
28 coffee pot
29 coffee cup
30 saucer
31 milk jug
32 sugar bowl
33 dinner set (dinner service)

1 dining table
2 tablecloth, a damask cloth
3–12 place (place setting, cover)
3 bottom plate
4 dinner plate
5 deep plate (soup plate)
6 dessert plate (dessert bowl)
7 knife and fork
8 fish knife and fork
9 serviette (napkin, table napkin)
10 serviette ring (napkin ring)
11 knife rest
12 wineglasses
13 place card
14 soup ladle
15 soup tureen (tureen)
16 candelabra
17 sauceboat (gravy boat)
18 sauce ladle (gravy ladle)
19 table decoration
20 bread basket
21 roll
22 slice of bread
23 salad bowl
24 salad servers
25 vegetable dish

26 meat plate (*Am.* meat platter)
27 roast meat (roast)
28 fruit dish
29 fruit bowl
30 fruit (stewed fruit)
31 potato dish
32 serving trolley
33 vegetable plate (*Am.* vegetable platter)
34 toast
35 cheeseboard
36 butter dish
37 open sandwich
38 filling
39 sandwich
40 fruit bowl
41 almonds (*also:* potato crisps, peanuts)
42 oil and vinegar bottle
43 ketchup (catchup, catsup)
44 sideboard
45 electric hotplate
46 corkscrew
47 crown cork bottle–opener (crown cork opener), a bottle-opener

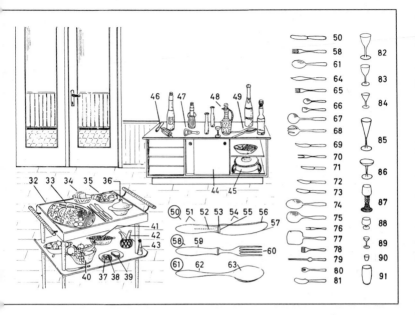

48 liqueur decanter
49 nutcrackers (nutcracker)
50 knife
51 handle
52 tang (tongue)
53 ferrule
54 blade
55 bolster
56 back
57 edge (cutting edge)
58 fork
59 handle
60 prong (tang, tine)
61 spoon; here: dessert spoon
62 handle
63 bowl
64 fish knife
65 fish fork
66 dessert spoon (fruit spoon)
67 salad spoon
68 salad fork
69–70 carving set (serving cutlery)
69 carving knife
70 serving fork
71 fruit knife
72 cheese knife

73 butter knife
74 vegetable spoon, a serving spoon
75 potato server (serving spoon for potatoes)
76 cocktail fork
77 asparagus server (asparagus slice)
78 sardine server
79 lobster fork
80 oyster fork
81 caviare knife
82 white wine glass
83 red wine glass
84 sherry glass (madeira glass)
85–86 champagne glasses
85 tapered glass
86 champagne glass, a crystal glass
87 rummer
88 brandy glass
89 liqueur glass
90 spirit glass
91 beer glass

46 Flat (Apartment)

1 wall units (shelf units)
2 wardrobe door (*Am.* clothes closet door)
3 body
4 side wall
5 trim
6 two-door cupboard unit
7 bookshelf unit (bookcase unit) [with glass door]
8 books
9 display cabinet
10 card index boxes
11 drawer
12 decorative biscuit tin
13 soft toy animal
14 television set (TV set)
15 records (discs)
16 bed unit
17 scatter cushion
18 bed unit drawer
19 bed unit shelf
20 magazines
21 desk unit (writing unit)
22 desk
23 desk mat (blotter)

24 table lamp
25 wastepaper basket
26 desk drawer
27 desk chair
28 arm
29 kitchen unit
30 wall cupboard
31 cooker hood
32 electric cooker
33 refrigerator (fridge, *Am.* icebox)
34 dining table
35 table runner
36 oriental carpet
37 standard lamp

1 children's bed, a bunk-bed
2 storage box
3 mattress
4 pillow
5 ladder
6 soft toy elephant, a cuddly toy animal
7 soft toy dog
8 cushion
9 fashion doll
10 doll's pram
11 sleeping doll
12 canopy
13 blackboard
14 counting beads
15 toy horse for rocking and pulling
16 rockers
17 children's book
18 compendium of games
19 ludo
20 chessboard
21 children's cupboard
22 linen drawer
23 drop-flap writing surface
24 notebook (exercise book)
25 school books
26 pencil (*also:* crayon, felt tip pen, ballpoint pen)
27 toy shop
28 counter
29 spice rack
30 display
31 assortment of sweets (*Am.* candies)
32 bag of sweets (*Am.* candies)
33 scales
34 cash register
35 toy telephone
36 shop shelves (goods shelves)
37 wooden train set
38 dump truck, a toy lorry (toy truck)
39 tower crane
40 concrete mixer
41 large soft toy dog
42 dice cup

48 Kindergarten (Day Nursery)

1–20 pre-school education
(nursery education)
1 nursery teacher
2 nursery child
3 handicraft
4 glue
5 watercolour (*Am.* watercolor) painting
6 paintbox
7 paintbrush
8 glass of water
9 jigsaw puzzle (puzzle)
10 jigsaw puzzle piece
11 coloured (*Am.* colored) pencils (wax crayons)
12 modelling (*Am.* modeling) clay (plasticine)
13 clay figures (plasticine figures)
14 modelling (*Am.* modeling) board
15 chalk (blackboard chalk)
16 blackboard
17 counting blocks
18 felt pen (felt tip pen)
19 shapes game
20 group of players
21–32 toys
21 building and filling cubes
22 construction set

23 children's books
24 doll's pram, a wicker pram
25 baby doll
26 canopy
27 building bricks (building blocks)
28 wooden model building
29 wooden train set
30 rocking teddy bear
31 doll's pushchair
32 fashion doll
33 child of nursery school age
34 cloakroom

1 bath	**25** overflow
2 mixer tap (*Am.* mixing faucet) for hot and cold water	**26** hot and cold water tap
3 foam bath (bubble bath)	**27** washbasin pedestal with trap (anti–syphon trap)
4 toy duck	**28** tooth glass (tooth mug)
5 bath salts	**29** electric toothbrush
6 bath sponge (sponge)	**30** detachable brush heads
7 bidet	**31** mirrored bathroom cabinet
8 towel rail	**32** fluorescent lamp
9 terry towel	**33** mirror
10 toilet roll holder (*Am.* bathroom tissue holder)	**34** drawer
11 toilet paper (*coll.* loo paper, *Am.* bathroom tissue), a roll of crepe paper	**35** powder box
	36 mouthwash
	37 electric shaver
12 toilet (lavatory, W.C., *coll.* loo)	**38** aftershave lotion
13 toilet pan (toilet bowl)	**39** shower cubicle
14 toilet lid with terry cover	**40** shower curtain
15 toilet seat	**41** adjustable shower head
16 cistern	**42** shower nozzle
17 flushing lever	**43** shower adjustment rail
18 pedestal mat	**44** shower base
19 tile	**45** waste pipe (overflow)
20 ventilator (extraction vent)	**46** bathroom mule
21 soap dish	**47** bathroom scales
22 soap	**48** bath mat
23 hand towel	**49** medicine cabinet
24 washbasin	

50 Household Appliances and Utensils

1–20 irons
1 electric ironing machine
2 electric foot switch
3 roller covering
4 ironing head
5 sheet
6 electric iron, a lightweight iron
7 sole–plate
8 temperature selector
9 handle (iron handle)
10 pilot light
11 steam, spray, and dry iron
12 filling inlet
13 spray nozzle for damping the washing
14 steam hole (steam slit)
15 ironing table
16 ironing board (ironing surface)
17 ironing–board cover
18 iron well
19 aluminium (*Am.* aluminum) frame
20 sleeve board
21 linen bin
22 dirty linen
23–34 washing machines and driers
23 washing machine (automatic washing machine)
24 washing drum
25 safety latch (safety catch)
26 program selector control
27 front soap dispenser [with several compartments]
28 tumble drier
29 drum
30 front door with ventilation slits
31 work top
32 airer
33 clothes line (washing line)
34 extending airer
35 stepladder (steps), an aluminium (*Am.* aluminum) ladder
36 stile
37 prop
38 tread (rung)
39–43 shoe care utensils
39 tin of shoe polish
40 shoe spray, an impregnating spray
41 shoe brush
42 brush for applying polish
43 tube of shoe polish
44 clothes brush

45 carpet brush
46 broom
47 bristles
48 broom head
49 broomstick (broom handle)
50 screw thread
51 washing–up brush
52 pan (dust pan)
53–86 floor and carpet cleaning
53 brush
54 bucket (pail)
55 floor cloth (cleaning rag)
56 scrubbing brush
57 carpet sweeper
58 upright vacuum cleaner
59 changeover switch
60 swivel head
61 bag–full indicator
62 dust bag container
63 handle
64 tubular handle
65 flex hook
66 wound–up flex
67 all–purpose nozzle
68 cylinder vacuum cleaner
69 swivel coupling
70 extension tube
71 floor nozzle (*sim.:* carpet beater nozzle)
72 suction control
73 bag–full indicator
74 sliding fingertip suction control
75 hose (suction hose)
76 combined carpet sweeper and shampooer
77 electric lead (flex)
78 plug socket
79 carpet beater head (*sim.:* shampooing head, brush head)
80 all–purpose vacuum cleaner (dry and wet operation)
81 castor
82 motor unit
83 lid clip
84 coarse dirt hose
85 special accessory (special attachment) for coarse dirt
86 dust container
87 shopper (shopping trolley)

1–35 flower garden
1 pergola
2 deck-chair
3 lawn rake (wire-tooth rake)
4 garden rake
5 Virginia creeper (American ivy, woodbine), a climbing plant (climber, creeper)
6 rockery (rock garden)
7 rock plants; *varieties:* stonecrop (wall pepper), houseleek, dryas, aubretia
8 pampas grass
9 garden hedge
10 blue spruce
11 hydrangeas
12 oak (oak tree)
13 birch (birch tree)
14 garden path
15 edging
16 garden pond
17 flagstone (stone slab)
18 water lily
19 tuberous begonias
20 dahlias

21 watering can (*Am.* sprinkling can)
22 weeding hoe
23 lupin
24 marguerites (oxeye daisies, white oxeye daisies)
25 standard rose
26 gerbera
27 iris
28 gladioli
29 chrysanthemums
30 poppy
31 blazing star
32 snapdragon (antirrhinum)
33 lawn
34 dandelion
35 sunflower

1–32 allotment (fruit and vegetable garden)

1, 2, 16, 17, 29 dwarf fruit trees (espaliers, espalier fruit trees)

1 quadruple cordon, a wall espalier
2 vertical cordon
3 tool shed (garden shed)
4 water butt (water barrel)
5 climbing plant (climber, creeper, rambler)
6 compost heap
7 sunflower
8 garden ladder (ladder)
9 perennial (flowering perennial)
10 garden fence (paling fence, paling)
11 standard berry tree
12 climbing rose (rambling rose) on the trellis arch
13 bush rose (standard rose tree)
14 summerhouse (garden house)
15 Chinese lantern (paper lantern)
16 pyramid tree (pyramidal tree, pyramid), a free-standing espalier

17 double horizontal cordon
18 flower bed, a border
19 berry bush (gooseberry bush, currant bush)
20 concrete edging
21 standard rose (standard rose tree)
22 border with perennials
23 garden path
24 allotment holder
25 asparagus patch (asparagus bed)
26 vegetable patch (vegetable plot)
27 scarecrow
28 runner bean (*Am.* scarlet runner), a bean plant on poles (bean poles)
29 horizontal cordon
30 standard fruit tree
31 tree stake
32 hedge

53 Indoor Plants (Houseplants)

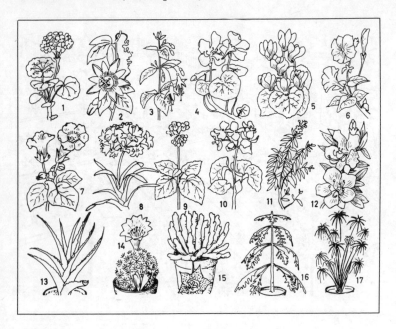

1 pelargonium (crane's bill), a
   geranium
2 passion flower (Passiflora), a
   climbing plant (climber, creeper)
3 fuchsia, an anagraceous plant
4 nasturtium (Indian cress,
   tropaeolum)
5 cyclamen, a primulaceous herb
6 petunia, a solanaceous herb
7 gloxinia (Sinningia), a
   gesneriaceous plant
8 Clivia minata, an amaryllis
   (narcissus)
9 African hemp (Sparmannia), a
   tiliaceous plant, a linden plant
10 begonia
11 myrtle (common myrtle, Myrtus)
12 azalea, an ericaceous plant
13 aloe, a liliaceous plant
14 globe thistle (Echinops)
15 stapelia (carrion flower), an
   asclepiadaceous plant

16 Norfolk Island Pine (an
   araucaria, grown as an
   ornamental)
17 galingale, a cyperacious plant of
   the sedge family

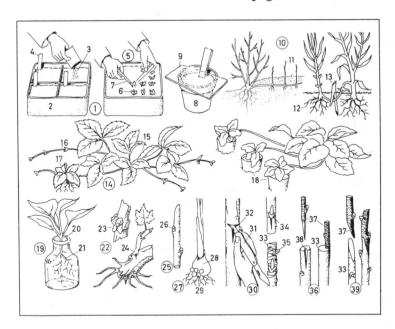

1 seed sowing (sowing)
2 seed pan
3 seed
4 label
5 pricking out (pricking off, transplanting)
6 seedling (seedling plant)
7 dibber (dibble)
8 flower pot (pot)
9 sheet of glass
10 propagation by layering
11 layer
12 layer with roots
13 forked stick used for fastening
14 propagation by runners
15 parent (parent plant)
16 runner
17 small rooted leaf cluster
18 setting in pots
19 cutting in water
20 cutting (slip, set)
21 root
22 bud cutting on vine tendril
23 scion bud, a bud
24 sprouting (shooting) cutting

25 stem cutting (hardwood cutting)
26 bud
27 propagation by bulbils (brood bud bulblets)
28 old bulb
29 bulbil (brood bud bulblet)
30–39 **grafting** (graftage)
30 budding (shield budding)
31 budding knife
32 T-cut
33 support (stock, rootstock)
34 inserted scion bud
35 raffia layer (bast layer)
36 side grafting
37 scion (shoot)
38 wedge–shaped notch
39 splice graft (splice grafting)

1–52 kinds of hunting
1–8 stalking (deer stalking, *Am.* stillhunting) in the game preserve
1 huntsman (hunter)
2 hunting clothes
3 knapsack
4 sporting gun (sporting rifle, hunting rifle)
5 huntsman's hat
6 field glasses, binoculars
7 gun dog
8 track (trail, hoofprints)
9–12 hunting in the rutting season and the pairing season
9 hunting screen (screen, *Am.* blind)
10 shooting stick (shooting seat, seat stick)
11 blackcock, displaying
12 rutting stag
13 hind, grazing

14–17 hunting from a raised hide (raised stand)
14 raised hide (raised stand, high seat)
15 herd within range
16 game path (*Am.* runway)
17 roebuck, hit in the shoulder and killed by a finishing shot
18 phaeton
19–27 types of trapping
19 trapping of small predators
20 box trap (trap for small predators)
21 bait
22 marten, a small predator
23 ferreting (hunting rabbits out of their warrens)
24 ferret
25 ferreter
26 burrow (rabbit burrow, rabbit hole)
27 net (rabbit net) over the burrow opening

28 feeding place for game (winter feeding place)
29 poacher
30 carbine, a short rifle
31 boar hunt
32 wild sow (sow, wild boar)
33 boarhound (hound, hunting dog; *collectively:* pack, pack of hounds)
34–39 beating (driving, hare hunting)
34 aiming position
35 hare, furred game, ground game
36 retrieving
37 beater
38 bag (kill)
39 cart for carrying game
40 waterfowling (wildfowling, duck shooting, *Am.* duck hunting)
41 flight of wild ducks, winged game

42–46 falconry (hawking)
42 falconer
43 reward, a piece of meat
44 falcon's hood
45 jess
46 falcon, a hawk, a male hawk (tiercel) swooping (stooping) on a heron
47–52 shooting from a butt
47 tree to which birds are lured
48 eagle owl, a decoy bird (decoy)
49 perch
50 decoyed bird, a crow
51 butt for shooting crows or eagle owls
52 gun slit

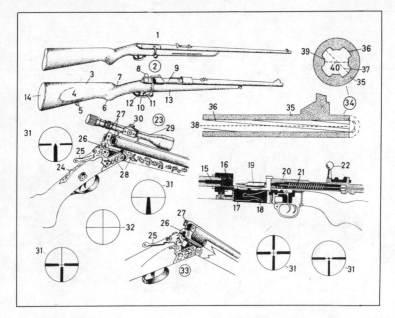

1-40 sporting guns (sporting rifles, hunting rifles)
1 single-loader (single-loading rifle)
2 repeating rifle, a small-arm (fire-arm), a repeater (magazine rifle, magazine repeater)
3, 4, 6, 13 stock
3 butt
4 cheek [on the left side]
5 sling ring
6 pistol grip
7 small of the butt
8 safety catch
9 lock
10 trigger guard
11 second set trigger (firing trigger)
12 hair trigger (set trigger)
13 foregrip
14 butt plate
15 cartridge chamber
16 receiver
17 magazine
18 magazine spring
19 ammunition (cartridge)
20 chamber
21 firing pin (striker)
22 bolt handle (bolt lever)
23 triple-barrelled (triple-barreled) rifle, a self-cocking gun
24 reversing catch (*in various guns:* safety catch)
25 sliding safety catch
26 rifle barrel (rifled barrel)
27 smooth-bore barrel
28 chasing
29 telescopic sight (riflescope, telescope sight)
30 graticule adjuster screws
31-32 graticule (sight graticule)
31 various graticule systems
32 cross wires (*Am.* cross hairs)
33 over-and-under shotgun
34 rifled gun barrel
35 barrel casing
36 rifling
37 rifling calibre (*Am.* caliber)
38 bore axis
39 land
40 calibre (bore diameter, *Am.* caliber)

41–48 hunting equipment
41 double–edged hunting knife
42 [single–edged] hunting knife
43–47 calls for luring game (for calling game)
43 roe call
44 hare call
45 quail call
46 stag call
47 partridge call
48 bow trap (bow gin), a jaw trap
49 small–shot cartridge
50 cardboard case
51 small–shot charge
52 felt wad
53 smokeless powder (*different kind:* black powder)
54 cartridge
55 full–jacketed cartridge
56 soft–lead core
57 powder charge
58 detonator cap
59 percussion cap
60 hunting horn
61–64 rifle cleaning kit
61 cleaning rod
62 cleaning brush
63 cleaning tow
64 pull–through (*Am.* pull–thru)
65 sights
66 notch (sighting notch)
67 back sight leaf
68 sight scale division
69 back sight slide
70 notch [to hold the spring]
71 front sight (foresight)
72 bead
73 ballistics
74 azimuth
75 angle of departure
76 angle of elevation
77 apex (zenith)
78 angle of descent
79 ballistic curve

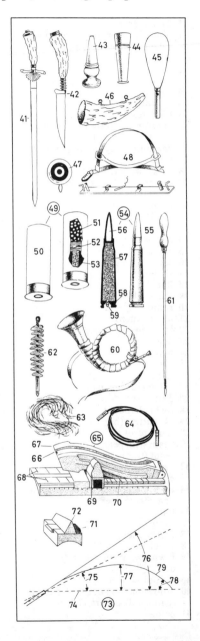

57 Game

1–27 red deer
1 hind (red deer), a young hind or a dam; *collectively:* anterless deer, *(y.)* calf
2 tongue
3 neck
4 rutting stag
5–11 antlers
5 burr (rose)
6 brow antler (brow tine, brow point, brow snag)
7 bez antler (bay antler, bay, bez tine)
8 royal antler (royal, tray)
9 surroyal antlers (surroyals)
10 point (tine)
11 beam (main trunk)
12 head
13 mouth
14 larmier (tear bag)
15 eye
16 ear
17 shoulder
18 loin
19 scut (tail)
20 rump
21 leg (haunch)
22 hind leg
23 dew claw
24 hoof
25 foreleg
26 flank
27 collar (rutting mane)
28–39 roe (roe deer)
28 roebuck (buck)
29–31 antlers (horns)
29 burr (rose)
30 beam with pearls
31 point (tine)
32 ear
33 eye
34 doe (female roe), a female fawn or a barren doe
35 loin
36 rump
37 leg (haunch)
38 shoulder
39 fawn, *(m.)* young buck, *(f.)* young doe
40–41 fallow deer
40 fallow buck, a buck with palmate (palmated) antlers, *(f.)* doe
41 palm

42 red fox, *(m.)* dog, *(f.)* vixen, *(y.)* cub
43 eyes
44 ear
45 muzzle (mouth)
46 pads (paws)
47 brush (tail)
48 badger, *(f.)* sow
49 tail
50 paws
51 wild boar, *(m.)* boar, *(f.)* wild sow (sow), *(y.)* young boar
52 bristles
53 snout
54 tusk
55 shield
56 hide
57 dew claw
58 tail
59 hare, *(m.)* buck, *(f.)* doe
60 eye
61 ear
62 scut (tail)
63 hind leg
64 foreleg
65 rabbit
66 blackcock
67 tail
68 falcate (falcated) feathers
69 hazel grouse (hazel hen)
70 partridge
71 horseshoe (horseshoe marking)
72 wood grouse (capercaillie)
73 beard
74 axillary marking
75 tail (fan)
76 wing (pinion)
77 common pheasant, a pheasant, *(m.)* cock pheasant (pheasant cock), *(f.)* hen pheasant (pheasant hen)
78 plumicorn (feathered ear, ear tuft, ear, horn)
79 wing
80 tail
81 leg
82 spur
83 snipe
84 bill (beak)

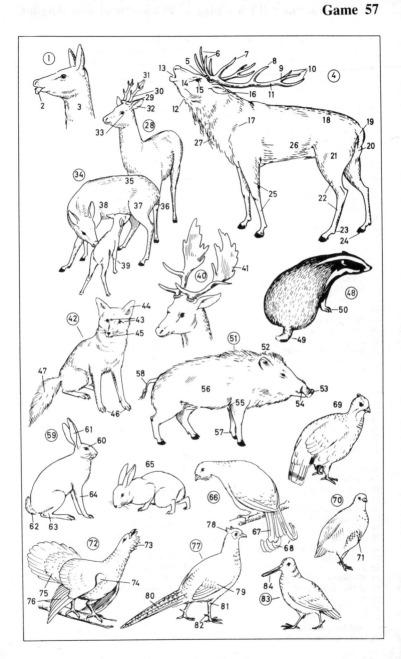

58 Fish Farming (Fish Culture, Pisciculture) and Angling

1-19 fish farming (fish culture, pisciculture)
1 cage in running water
2 hand net (landing net)
3 semi-oval barrel for transporting fish
4 vat
5 trellis in the overflow
6 trout pond; *sim.:* carp pond, a fry pond, fattening pond, or cleansing pond
7 water inlet (water supply pipe)
8 water outlet (outlet pipe)
9 monk
10 screen
11-19 hatchery
11 stripping the spawning pike (seed pike)
12 fish spawn (spawn, roe, fish eggs)
13 female fish (spawner, seed fish)
14 trout breeding (trout rearing)
15 Californian incubator
16 trout fry
17 hatching jar for pike
18 long incubation tank
19 Brandstetter egg-counting board
20-94 angling
20-31 coarse fishing
20 line shooting
21 coils
22 cloth (rag) or paper
23 rod rest
24 bait tin
25 fish basket (creel)
26 fishing for carp from a boat
27 rowing boat (fishing boat)
28 keep net
29 drop net
30 pole (punt pole, quant pole)
31 casting net
32 two-handed side cast with fixed-spool reel
33 initial position
34 point of release
35 path of the rod tip
36 trajectory of the baited weight
37-94 fishing tackle
37 fishing pliers
38 filleting knife
39 fish knife
40 disgorger (hook disgorger)
41 bait needle
42 gag
43-48 floats
43 sliding cork float
44 plastic float
45 quill float
46 polystyrene float
47 oval bubble float
48 lead-weighted sliding float

49-58 rods
49 solid glass rod
50 cork handle (cork butt)
51 spring-steel ring
52 top ring (end ring)
53 telescopic rod
54 rod section
55 bound handle (bound butt)
56 ring
57 carbon-fibre rod; *sim.:* hollow glass rod
58 all-round ring (butt ring for long cast), a steel bridge ring
59-64 reels
59 multiplying reel (multiplier reel)
60 line guide
61 fixed-spool reel (stationary-drum reel)
62 bale arm
63 fishing line
64 controlling the cast with the index finger
65-76 baits
65 fly
66 artificial nymph
67 artificial earthworm
68 artificial grasshopper
69 single-jointed plug (single-jointed wobbler)
70 double-jointed plug (double-jointed wobbler)
71 round wobbler
72 wiggler
73 spoon bait (spoon)
74 spinner
75 spinner with concealed hook
76 long spinner
77 swivel
78 cast (leader)
79-87 hooks
79 fish hook
80 point of the hook with barb
81 bend of the hook
82 spade (eye)
83 open double hook
84 limerick
85 closed treble hook (triangle)
86 carp hook
87 eel hook
88-92 leads (lead weights)
88 oval lead (oval sinker)
89 lead shot
90 pear-shaped lead
81 plummet
92 sea lead
93 fish ladder (fish pass, fish way)
94 stake net

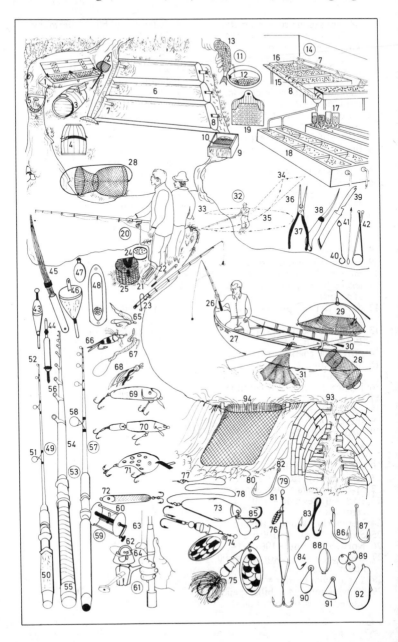

59 Money (Coins and Notes, *Am.* Coins and Bills)

1-28 **coins** (coin, coinage, metal
  money, specie, *Am.* hard money;
  kinds: gold, silver, nickel,
  copper, or aluminium, *Am.*
  aluminum, coins)
1 Athens: nugget–shaped
  tetradrachm (tetradrachmon,
  tetradrachma)
2 the owl (emblem of the city of
  Athens)
3 aureus of Constantine the Great
4 bracteate of Emperor Frederick I
  Barbarossa
5 Louis XIV louis–d'or
6 Prussia: 1 reichstaler
  (speciestaler) of Frederick the
  Great
7 Federal Republic of Germany: 5
  Deutschmarks (DM); 1 DM =
  100 pfennigs
8 obverse
9 reverse (subordinate side)
10 mint mark (mintage, exergue)
11 legend (inscription on the edge
  of a coin)
12 device (type), a provincial coat of
  arms
13 Austria: 25 schillings; 1 sch =
  100 groschen
14 provincial coats of arms
15 Switzerland: 5 francs; 1 franc =
  100 centimes
16 France: 1 franc = 100 centimes
17 Belgium: 100 francs
18 Luxembourg (Luxemburg): 1
  franc
19 Netherlands: $2\frac{1}{2}$ guilders; 1
  guilder (florin, gulden) = 100
  cents
20 Italy: 10 lire (*sg.* lira)
21 Vatican City: 10 lire (*sg.* lira)
22 Spain: 1 peseta = 100 céntimos
23 Portugal: 1 escudo = 100
  centavos
24 Denmark: 1 krone = 100 öre
25 Sweden: 1 krona = 100 öre
26 Norway: 1 krone = 100 öre
27 Czechoslovakia: 1 koruna = 100
  heller
28 Yugoslavia: 1 dinar = 100 paras
29-39 **banknotes** (*Am.* bills) (paper
  money, notes, treasury notes)

29 Federal Republic of Germany:
  20 DM
30 bank of issue (bank of
  circulation)
31 watermark [a portrait]
32 denomination
33 USA: 1 dollar($1) = 100 cents
34 facsimile signatures
35 impressed stamp
36 serial number
37 United Kingdom of Great
  Britain and Northern Ireland: 1
  pound sterling (£1) = 100 new
  pence (100p.; *sg.* new penny
  (new p.)
38 guilloched pattern
39 Greece: 1,000 drachmas
  (drachmae); 1 drachma = 100
  lepta (*sg.* lepton)
40-44 **striking of coins** (coinage,
  mintage)
40-41 coining dies (minting dies)
40 upper die
41 lower die
42 collar
43 coin disc (disk) (flan, planchet,
  blank)
44 coining press (minting press)

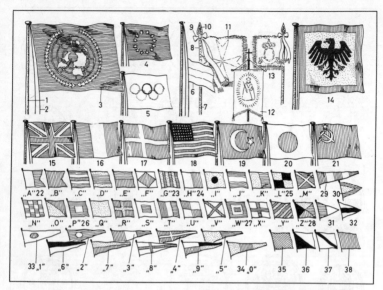

1-3 flag of the United Nations
1 flagpole (flagstaff) with truck
2 halyard (halliard, haulyard)
3 bunting
4 flag of the Council of Europe
5 Olympic flag
6 flag at half-mast (*Am*. at half-staff) [as a token of mourning]
7-11 flag
7 flagpole (flagstaff)
8 ornamental stud
9 streamer
10 pointed tip of the flagpole
11 bunting
12 banner (gonfalon)
13 cavalry standard (flag of the cavalry)
14 standard of the German Federal President [ensign of head of state]
15-21 national flags
15 the Union Jack (Great Britain)
16 the Tricolour (*Am*. Tricolor) (France)
17 the Danebrog (Dannebrog) (Denmark)
18 the Stars and Stripes (Star-Spangled Banner) (USA)
19 the Crescent (Turkey)
20 the Rising Sun (Japan)
21 the Hammer and Sickle (USSR)

22-34 signal flags, a hoist
22-28 letter flags
22 letter A, a burgee (swallow-tailed flag)
23 G, pilot flag
24 H ('pilot on board')
25 L ('you should stop, I have something important to communicate')
26 P, the Blue Peter ('about to set sail')
27 W ('I require medical assistance')
28 Z, an oblong pennant (oblong pendant)
29 code pennant (code pendant), used in the International Signals Code
30-32 substitute flags (repeaters), triangular flags (pennants, pendants)
33-34 numeral pennants (numeral pendants)
33 number 1
34 number 0
35-38 customs flags
35 customs boat pennant (customs boat pendant)
36 'ship cleared through customs'
37 customs signal flag
38 powder flag ['inflammable (flammable) cargo']

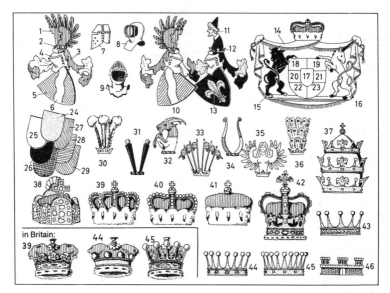

1-36 heraldry (blazonry)
1, 11, 30-36 crests
1-6 coat-of-arms (achievement of arms, hatchment, achievement)
1 crest
2 wreath of the colours (*Am.* colors)
3 mantle (mantling)
4, 7-9 helmets (helms)
4 tilting helmet (jousting helmet)
5 shield
6 bend sinister wavy
7 pot-helmet (pot-helm, heaume)
8 barred helmet (grilled helmet)
9 helmet affronty with visor open
10-13 marital achievement (marshalled, *Am.* marshaled, coat-of-arms)
10 arms of the baron (of the husband)
11-13 arms of the family of the femme (of the wife)
11 demi-man; *also:* demi-woman
12 crest coronet
13 fleur-de-lis
14 mantling
15-16 supporters (heraldic beasts)
15 bull
16 unicorn
17-23 blazon
17 inescutcheon (heart-shield)
18-23 quarterings one to six
18, 20, 22 dexter, right

18-19 chief
19, 21, 23 sinister, left
22-23 base
24-29 tinctures
24-25 metals
24 or (gold) [yellow]
25 argent (silver) [white]
26 sable
27 gules
28 azure
29 vert
30 ostrich feathers (treble plume)
31 truncheon
32 demi-goat
33 tournament pennons
34 buffalo horns
35 harpy
36 plume of peacock's feathers
37-46 crowns and coronets
37 tiara (papal tiara)
38 Imperial Crown [German, until 1806]
39 ducal coronet (duke's coronet)
40 prince's coronet
41 elector's coronet
42 English Royal Crown
43-45 coronets of rank
43 baronet's coronet
44 baron's coronet (baronial coronet)
45 count's coronet
46 mauerkrone (mural crown) of a city crest

62 Armed Forces I (Army)

1-98 army weaponry
1-39 **hand weapons**
1 Pl pistol
2 barrel
3 front sight (foresight)
4 hammer
5 trigger
6 pistol grip
7 magazine holder
8 MP2 machine gun
9 shoulder rest (butt)
10 casing (mechanism casing)
11 barrel clamp (barrel-clamping nut)
12 cocking lever (cocking handle)
13 palm rest
14 safety catch
15 magazine
16 G3-A3 self-loading rifle
17 barrel
18 flash hider (flash eliminator)
19 palm rest
20 trigger mechanism
21 magazine
22 notch (sighting notch, rearsight)
23 front sight block (foresight block)
   with front sight (foresight)
24 rifle butt (butt)
25 44 mm anti-tank rocket launcher
26 rocket (projectile)
27 buffer
28 telescopic sight (telescope sight)
29 firing mechanism
30 cheek rest
31 shoulder rest (butt)
32 MG3 machine gun (Spandau)
33 barrel casing
34 gas regulator
35 belt-changing flap
36 rearsight
37 front sight block (foresight block)
   with front sight (foresight)
38 pistol grip
39 shoulder rest (butt)
40-95 **heavy weapons**
40 120 mm AM 50 mortar
41 barrel
42 bipod
43 gun carriage
44 buffer (buffer ring)
45 sight (sighting mechanism)
46 base plate
47 striker pad
48 traversing handle
49-74 artillery weapons mounted
   on self-propelled gun carriages
49 175 mm SFM 107 cannon
50 drive wheel

51 elevating piston
52 buffer (buffer recuperator)
53 hydraulic system
54 breech ring
55 spade
56 spade piston
57 155 mm M 109 G self-propelled gun
58 muzzle
59 fume extractor
60 barrel cradle
61 barrel recuperator
62 barrel clamp
63 light anti-aircraft (AA) machine gun
64 Honest John M 386 rocket
   launcher
65 rocket with warhead
66 launching ramp
67 elevating gear
68 jack
69 cable winch
70 110 SF rocket launcher
71 disposable rocket tubes
72 tube bins
73 turntable
74 fire control system
75 2.5 tonne construction vehicle
76 lifting arms (lifting device)
77 shovel
78 counterweight (counterpoise)
79-95 **armoured** (*Am.* **armored**)
   vehicles
79 M 113 armoured (*Am.* armored)
   ambulance
80 Leopard 1 A 3 tank
81 protection device
82 infrared laser rangefinder
83 smoke canisters (smoke
   dispensers)
84 armoured (*Am.* armored) turret
85 skirt
86 road wheel
87 track
88 anti-tank tank
89 fume extractor
90 protection device
91 armoured (*Am.* armored)
   personnel carrier
92 cannon
93 armoured (*Am.* armored)
   recovery vehicle
94 levelling (*Am.* leveling) and
   support shovel
95 jib
96 25 tonne all-purpose vehicle
97 drop windscreen (*Am.* drop
   windshield)
98 canvas cover

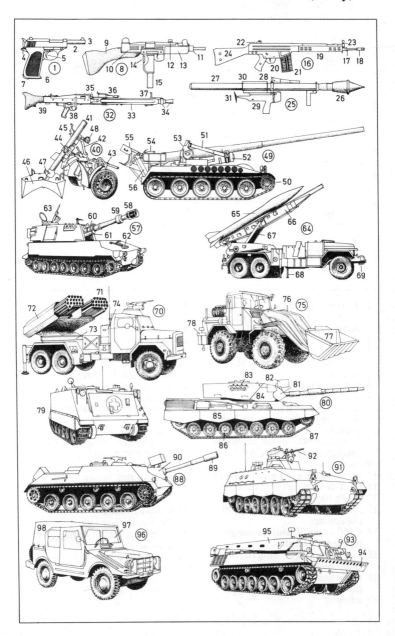

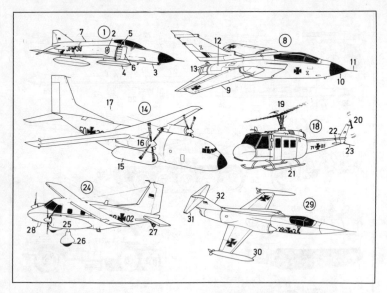

1 *McDonnell–Douglas F–4F Phantom II* **interceptor and fighter–bomber**
2 squadron marking
3 aircraft cannon
4 wing tank (underwing tank)
5 air intake
6 boundary layer control flap
7 in-flight refuelling (*Am.* refueling) probe (flight refuelling probe, air refuelling probe)
8 *Panavia 2000 Tornado* **multirole combat aircraft** (MRCA)
9 swing wing
10 radar nose (radome, radar dome)
11 pitot–static tube (pitot tube)
12 brake flap (air brake)
13 afterburner exhaust nozzles of the engines
14 *C160 Transall* **medium–range transport aircraft**
15 undercarriage housing (landing gear housing)
16 propeller–turbine engine (turboprop engine)
17 antenna

18 *Bell UH–ID Iroquois* **light transport and rescue helicopter**
19 main rotor
20 tail rotor
21 landing skids
22 stabilizing fins (stabilizing surfaces, stabilizers)
23 tail skid
24 *Dornier DO 28 D–2 Skyservant* **transport and communications aircraft**
25 engine pod
26 main undercarriage unit (main landing gear unit)
27 tail wheel
28 sword antenna
29 *F–104 G Starfighter* **fighter–bomber**
30 wing–tip tank (tip tank)
31–32 T–tail (T–tail unit)
31 tailplane (horizontal stabilizer, stabilizer)
32 vertical stabilizer (vertical fin, tail fin)

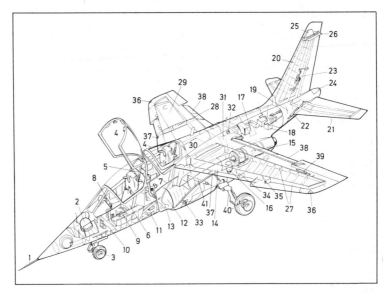

1–41 *Dornier–Dassault–Breguet Alpha Jet* Franco–German jet trainer
1 pitot–static tube (pitot tube)
2 oxygen tank
3 forward–retracting nose wheel
4 cockpit canopy (cockpit hood)
5 canopy jack
6 pilot's seat (student pilot's seat), an ejector seat (ejection seat)
7 observer's seat (instructor's seat), an ejector seat (ejection seat)
8 control column (control stick)
9 thrust lever
10 rudder pedals with brakes
11 front avionics bay
12 air intake to the engine
13 boundary layer control flap
14 air intake duct
15 turbine engine
16 reservoir for the hydraulic system
17 battery housing
18 rear avionics bay
19 baggage compartment
20 triple–spar tail construction
21 horizontal tail
22 servo–actuating mechanism for the elevator
23 servo–actuating mechanism for the rudder
24 brake chute housing (drag chute housing)
25 VHF (very high frequency) antenna (UHF antenna)
26 VOR (very high frequency omnidirectional range) antenna
27 twin–spar wing construction
28 former with integral spars
29 integral wing tanks
30 centre–section (*Am.* center–section) fuel tank
31 fuselage tanks
32 gravity fuelling (*Am.* fueling) point
33 pressure fuelling (*Am.* fueling) point
34 inner wing suspension
35 outer wing suspension
36 navigation lights (position lights)
37 landing lights
38 landing flap
39 aileron actuator
40 forward–retracting main undercarriage unit (main landing gear unit)
41 undercarriage hydraulic cylinder (landing gear hydraulic cylinder)

65 Warships I (Navy)

1-63 light battleships
1 destroyer
2 hull of flush-deck vessel
3 bow (stem)
4 flagstaff (jackstaff)
5 anchor, a stockless anchor (patent anchor)
6 anchor capstan (windlass)
7 breakwater (*Am.* manger board)
8 chine strake
9 main deck
10-28 superstructures
10 superstructure deck
11 life rafts
12 cutter (ship's boat)
13 davit (boat-launching crane)
14 bridge (bridge superstructure)
15 side navigation light (side running light)
16 antenna
17 radio direction finder (RDF) frame
18 lattice mast
19 forward funnel
20 aft funnel
21 cowl
22 aft superstructure (poop)
23 capstan
24 companion ladder (companionway, companion hatch)
25 ensign staff
26 stern, a transom stern
27 waterline
28 searchlight
29-37 armament
29 100 mm gun turret
30 four-barrel anti-submarine rocket launcher (missile launcher)
31 40 mm twin anti-aircraft (AA) gun
32 MM 38 anti-aircraft (AA) rocket launcher (missile launcher) in launching container
33 anti-submarine torpedo tube
34 depth-charge thrower
35 weapon system radar
36 radar antenna (radar scanner)
37 optical rangefinder
38 destroyer
39 bower anchor
40 propeller guard
41 tripod lattice mast
42 pole mast
43 ventilator openings (ventilator grill)
44 exhaust pipe
45 ship's boat
46 antenna
47 radar-controlled 127 mm all-purpose gun in turret

48 127 mm all-purpose gun
49 launcher for Tartar missiles
50 anti-submarine rocket (ASROC) launcher (missile launcher)
51 fire control radar antennas
52 radome (radar dome)
53 frigate
54 hawse pipe
55 steaming light
56 navigation light (running light)
57 air extractor duct
58 funnel
59 cowl
60 whip antenna (fishpole antenna)
61 cutter
62 stern light
63 propeller guard boss
64-91 fighting ships
64 submarine
65 flooded foredeck
66 pressure hull
67 turret
68 retractable instruments
69 E-boat (torpedo boat)
70 76 mm all-purpose gun with turret
71 missile-launching housing
72 deckhouse
73 40 mm anti-aircraft (AA) gun
74 propeller guard moulding (*Am.* molding)
75 143 class E-boat (143 class torpedo boat)
76 breakwater (*Am.* manger board)
77 radome (radar dome)
78 torpedo tube
79 exhaust escape flue
80 mine hunter
81 reinforced rubbing strake
82 inflatable boat (inflatable dinghy)
83 davit
84 minesweeper
85 cable winch
86 towing winch (towing machine, towing engine)
87 mine-sweeping gear (paravanes)
88 crane (davit)
89 landing craft
90 bow ramp
91 stern ramp
92-97 auxiliaries
92 tender
93 servicing craft
94 minelayer
95 training ship
96 deep-sea salvage tug
97 fuel tanker (replenishing ship)

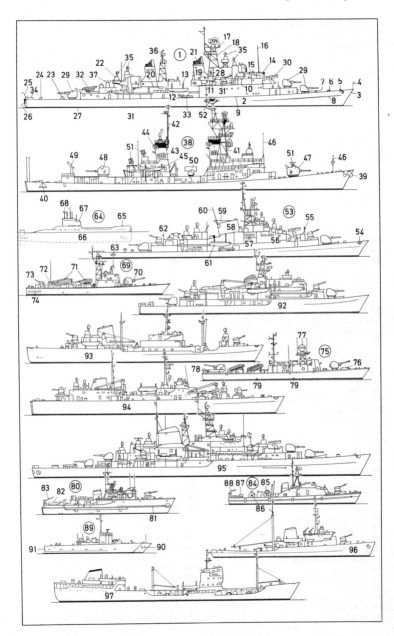

66 Warships II (Modern Fighting Ships)

1 **nuclear-powered aircraft carrier**
   '*Nimitz ICVN68*' (USA)
2-11 body plan
2 flight deck
3 island (bridge)
4 aircraft lift (*Am*. aircraft elevator)
5 eight-barrel anti-aircraft (AA)
   rocket launcher (missile
   launcher)
6 pole mast (antenna mast)
7 antenna
8 radar antenna (radar scanner)
8 fully enclosed bow
10 deck crane
11 transom stern
12-20 deck plan
12 angle deck (flight deck)
13 aircraft lift (*Am*. aircraft elevator)
14 twin launching catapult
15 hinged (movable) baffle board
16 arrester wire
17 emergency crash barrier
18 safety net
19 caisson (cofferdam)
20 eight-barrel anti-aircraft (AA)
   rocket launcher (missile launcher)
21 '*Kara*' class **rocket cruiser**
   (missile cruiser) (USSR)
22 hull of flush–deck vessel
23 sheer
24 twelve-barrel underwater salvo
   rocket launcher (missile launcher)
25 twin anti-aircraft (AA) rocket
   launcher (missile launcher)
26 launching housing for 4 short-range
   rockets (missiles)
27 baffle board
28 bridge
29 radar antenna (radar scanner)
30 twin 76 mm anti-aircraft (AA)
   gun turret
31 turret
32 funnel
33 twin anti-aircraft (AA) rocket
   launcher (missile launcher)
34 automatic anti-aircraft (AA) gun
35 ship's boat
36 underwater 5-torpedo housing
37 underwater 6-salvo rocket
   launcher (missile launcher)
38 helicopter hangar
39 helicopter landing platform
40 variable depth sonar (VDS)
41 '*California*' class **rocket cruiser**
   (missile cruiser) (USA)
42 hull
43 forward turret
44 aft turret
45 forward superstructure
46 landing craft
47 antenna

48 radar antenna (radar scanner)
49 radome (radar dome)
50 surface-to-air rocket launcher
   (missile launcher)
51 underwater rocket launcher
   (missile launcher)
52 127 mm gun with turret
53 helicopter landing platform
54 **nuclear-powered fleet**
   submarine
55-74 middle section [diagram]
55 pressure hull
56 auxiliary engine room
57 rotary turbine pump
58 steam turbine generator
59 propeller shaft
60 thrust block
61 reduction gear
62 high and low pressure turbine
63 high-pressure steam pipe for the
   secondary water circuit
   (auxiliary water circuit)
64 condenser
65 primary water circuit
66 heat exchanger
67 nuclear reactor casing (atomic
   pile casing)
68 reactor core
69 control rods
70 lead screen
71 turret
72 snorkel (schnorkel)
73 air inlet
74 retractable instruments
75 **patrol submarine** with
   conventional (diesel-electric)
   drive
76 pressure hull
77 flooded foredeck
78 outer flap (outer doors) [for
   torpedoes]
79 torpedo tube
80 bow bilge
81 anchor
82 anchor winch
83 battery
84 living quarters with folding bunks
85 commanding officer's cabin
86 main hatchway
87 flagstaff
88-91 retractable instruments
88 attack periscope
89 antenna
90 snorkel (schnorkel)
91 radar antenna (radar scanner)
92 exhaust outlet
93 heat space (hot-pipe space)
94 diesel generators
95 aft diving plane and vertical
   rudder
96 forward vertical rudder

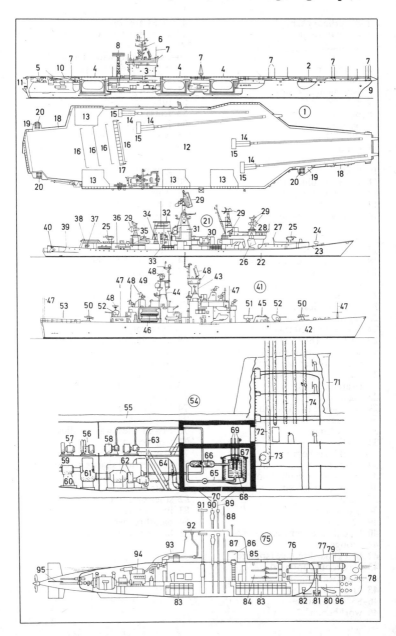

67 School I (Primary School)

1–85 primary school
1–45 classroom
1 arrangement of desks in a horseshoe
2 double desk
3 pupils (children) in a group (sitting in a group)
4 exercise book
5 pencil
6 wax crayon
7 school bag
8 handle
9 school satchel (satchel)
10 front pocket
11 strap (shoulder strap)
12 pen and pencil case
13 zip
14 fountain pen (pen)
15 loose–leaf file (ring file)
16 reader
17 spelling book
18 notebook (exercise book)
19 felt tip pen
20 pupil raising her hand
21 teacher
22 teacher's desk
23 register
24 pen and pencil tray
25 desk mat (blotter)
26 window painting with finger paints (finger painting)
27 pupils' (children's) paintings (watercolours)
28 cross
29 three–part blackboard
30 bracket for holding charts
31 chalk ledge
32 chalk
33 blackboard drawing
34 diagram
35 reversible side blackboard
36 projection screen
37 triangle
38 protractor
39 divisions
40 blackboard compass
41 sponge tray
42 blackboard sponge (sponge)
43 classroom cupboard
44 map (wall map)
45 brick wall
46–85 craft room
46 workbench

47 vice (*Am.* vise)
48 vice (*Am.* vise) bar
49 scissors
50–52 working with glue (sticking paper, cardboard, etc.)
50 surface to be glued
51 tube of glue
52 tube cap
53 fretsaw
54 fretsaw blade (saw blade)
55 wood rasp (rasp)
56 piece of wood held in the vice (*Am.* vise)
57 glue pot
58 stool
59 brush
60 pan (dust pan)
61 broken china
62 enamelling (*Am.* enameling)
63 electric enamelling (*Am.* enameling) stove
64 unworked copper
65 enamel powder
66 hair sieve
67–80 pupils' (children's) work
67 clay models (models)
68 window decoration of coloured (*Am.* colored) glass
69 glass mosaic picture (glass mosaic)
70 mobile
71 paper kite (kite)
72 wooden construction
73 polyhedron
74 hand puppets
75 clay masks
76 cast candles (wax candles)
77 wood carving
78 clay jug
79 geometrical shapes made of clay
80 wooden toys
81 materials
82 stock of wood
83 inks for wood cuts
84 paintbrushes
85 bag of plaster of Paris

68 School II (Secondary School, High School)

1-45 grammar school; *also:* upper band of a comprehensive school (*Am.* alternative school)

1-13 chemistry
1 chemistry lab (chemistry laboratory) with tiered rows of seats
2 chemistry teacher
3 demonstration bench (teacher's bench)
4 water pipe
5 tiled working surface
6 sink
7 television monitor, a screen for educational programmes (*Am.* programs)
8 overhead projector
9 projector top for skins
10 projection lens with right–angle mirror
11 pupils' (*Am.* students') bench with experimental apparatus
12 electrical point (socket)
13 projection table
14-34 biology preparation room (biology prep room)
14 skeleton
15 casts of skulls
16 calvarium of Pithecanthropus Erectus
17 skull of Steinheim man
18 calvarium of Peking man (of Sinanthropus)
19 skull of Neanderthal man, a skull of primitive man
20 Australopithecine skull (skull of Australopithecus)
21 skull of present–day man
22 dissecting bench
23 chemical bottles
24 gas tap
25 petri dish
26 measuring cylinder
27 work folder (teaching material)
28 textbook
29 bacteriological cultures
30 incubator
31 test tube rack
32 washing bottle
33 water tank
34 sink
35 language laboratory
36 blackboard

37 console
38 headphones (headset)
39 microphone
40 earcups
41 padded headband (padded headpiece)
42 programme (*Am.* program) recorder, a cassette recorder
43 pupil's (*Am.* student's) volume control
44 master volume control
45 control buttons (operating keys)

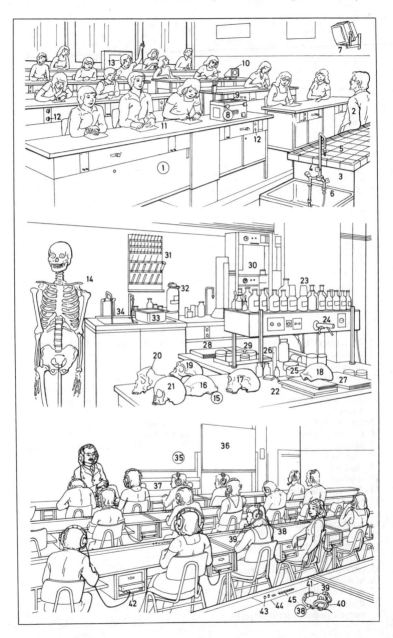

69 University

1–25 **university** (college)
1 lecture
2 lecture room (lecture theatre, *Am.* theater)
3 university lecturer (lecturer, *Am.* assistant professor)
4 lectern
5 lecture notes
6 demonstrator
7 assistant
8 diagram
9 student
10 student
11–25 **university library**
11 stack (book stack) with the stock of books
12 bookshelf, a steel shelf
13 reading room
14 member of the reading room staff, a librarian
15 periodicals rack with periodicals
16 newspaper shelf
17 reference library with reference books (handbooks, encyclopedias, dictionaries)
18 lending library and catalogue (*Am.* catalog) room
19 librarian
20 issue desk
21 main catalogue (*Am.* catalog)
22 card catalogue (*Am.* catalog)
23 card catalogue (*Am.* catalog) drawer
24 library user
25 borrower's ticket (library ticket)

1–15 election meeting, a public meeting
1–2 committee
1 chairman
2 committee member
3 committee table
4 bell
5 election speaker (speaker)
6 rostrum
7 microphone
8 meeting (audience)
9 man distributing leaflets
10 stewards
11 armband (armlet)
12 banner
13 placard
14 proclamation
15 heckler
16–30 election
16 polling station (polling place)
17 election officer
18 electoral register
19 polling card with registration number (polling number)

20 ballot paper with the names of the parties and candidates
21 ballot envelope
22 voter
23 polling booth
24 elector (qualified voter)
25 election regulations
26 clerk
27 clerk with the duplicate list
28 election supervisor
29 ballot box
30 slot

71 Police

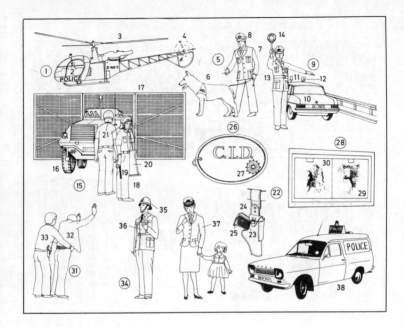

1–33 **police duties**
1 **police helicopter** (traffic helicopter) for controlling (*Am.* controling) traffic from the air
2 cockpit
3 rotor (main rotor)
4 tail rotor
5 **police dog and handler**
6 police dog
7 uniform
8 uniform cap, a peaked cap with cockade
9 **traffic control by a mobile traffic patrol**
10 patrol car
11 blue light
12 loud hailer (loudspeaker)
13 patrolman (police patrolman)
14 police signalling (*Am.* signaling) disc (disk)
15 **riot duty**
16 special armoured (*Am.* armored) car
17 barricade
18 policeman (police officer) in riot gear
19 truncheon (baton)
20 riot shield
21 protective helmet (helmet)
22 **service pistol**
23 pistol grip
24 quick–draw holster
25 magazine
26 **police identification disc (disk)**
27 police badge
28 **fingerprint identification** (dactyloscopy)
29 fingerprint
30 illuminated screen
31 **search**
32 suspect
33 detective (plainclothes policeman)
34 English policeman
35 helmet
36 pocket book
37 policewoman
38 police van

120

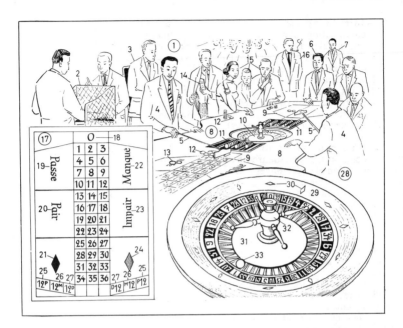

1–33 **roulette**, a game of chance (gambling game)
1 gaming room in a casino (gambling casino)
2 cash desk
3 tourneur (dealer)
4 croupier
5 rake
6 head croupier
7 hall manager
8 roulette table (gaming table, gambling table)
9 roulette layout
10 roulette wheel
11 bank
12 chip (check, plaque)
13 stake
14 membership card
15 roulette player
16 private detective (house detective)
17 roulette layout
18 zero (nought, O)
19 passe (high) [numbers 19 to 36]

20 pair (even numbers)
21 noir (black)
22 manque (low) [numbers 1 to 18]
23 impair [odd numbers]
24 rouge (red)
25 douze premier (first dozen) [numbers 1 to 12]
26 douze milieu (second dozen) [numbers 13 to 24]
27 douze dernier (third dozen) [numbers 25 to 36]
28 roulette wheel (roulette)
29 roulette bowl
30 fret (separator)
31 revolving disc (disk) showing numbers 0 to 36
32 spin
33 roulette ball

73 Board Games and Party Games

1–16 **chess,** a game involving combinations of moves, a positional game
1 chessboard (board) with the men (chessmen) in position
2 white square (chessboard square)
3 black square
4 white chessmen (white pieces) [white = W]
5 black chessmen (black pieces) [black = B]
6 letters and numbers for designating chess squares in the notation of chess moves and chess problems
7 individual chessmen (individual pieces)
8 king
9 queen
10 bishop
11 knight
12 rook (castle)
13 pawn
14 moves of the individual pieces
15 mate (checkmate), a mate by knight
16 chess clock, a double clock for chess matches (chess championships)
17–19 **draughts** (*Am.* checkers)
17 draughtboard (*Am.* checkerboard)
18 white draughtsman (*Am.* checker, checkerman); *also:* piece for backgammon and nine men's morris
19 black draughtsman (*Am.* checker, checkerman)
20 **salta**
21 salta piece
22 backgammon board
23–25 **nine men's morris**
23 nine men's morris board
24 mill
25 double mill
26–28 **halma**
26 halma board
27 yard (camp, corner)
28 halma pieces (halma men) of various colours (*Am.* colors)
29 **dice** (dicing)
30 dice cup
31 dice

32 spots (pips)
33 **dominoes**
34 domino (tile)
35 double
36 **playing cards**
37 playing card (card)
38–45 suits
38 clubs
39 spades
40 hearts
41 diamonds
42–45 German suits
42 acorns
43 leaves
44 hearts
45 bells (hawkbells)

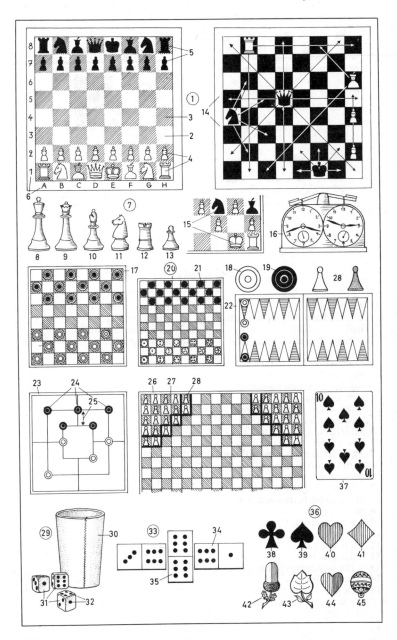

74 Billiards

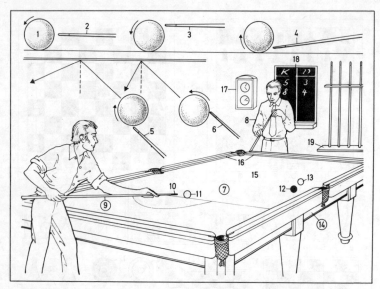

1–19 billiards
1 billiard ball, an ivory or plastic ball
2–6 billiard strokes (forms of striking)
2 plain stroke (hitting the cue ball dead centre, *Am.* center)
3 top stroke [promotes extra forward rotation]
4 screw–back [imparts a direct recoil or backward motion]
5 side (running side, *Am.* English)
6 check side
7–19 billiard room (*Am.* billiard parlor, billiard saloon, poolroom)
7 billiards (English billiards); *sim.:* pool, carom (carrom) billiards
8 billiard player
9 billiard cue (cue)
10 leather cue tip
11 white cue ball
12 red object ball
13 white spot ball (white dot ball)
14 billiard table
15 table bed with green cloth (billiard cloth, green baize covering)

16 cushions (rubber cushions, cushioned ledge)
17 billiard clock, a timer
18 billiard marker
19 cue rack

1-59 **camp site**
(camping site,
Am. campground)
1 reception (office)
2 camp site attendant
3 folding trailer
(collapsible caravan,
collapsible trailer)
4 hammock
5-6 washing and toilet
facilities
5 toilets and washrooms
(*Am.* lavatories)
6 washbasins and sinks
7 bungalow (chalet)
8-11 **scout camp**
8 bell tent
9 pennon
10 camp fire
11 boy scout (scout)
12 sailing boat (yacht,
Am. sailboat)
13 landing stage (jetty)
14 inflatable boat
(inflatable dinghy)
15 outboard motor
(outboard)

16 trimaran
17 thwart (oarsman's
bench)
18 rowlock (oarlock)
19 oar
20 boat trailer (boat
carriage)
21 **ridge tent**
22 flysheet
23 guy line (guy)
24 tent peg (peg)
25 mallet
26 groundsheet ring
27 bell end
28 erected awning
29 storm lantern,
a paraffin lamp
30 sleeping bag
31 air mattress
(inflatable air-bed)
32 water carrier
(drinking water carrier)
33 double-burner gas
cooker for propane gas
or butane gas
34 propane or butane
gas bottle

35 pressure cooker
36 **frame tent**
37 awning
38 tent pole
39 wheelarch doorway
40 mesh ventilator
41 transparent window
42 pitch number
43 folding camp chair
44 folding camp table
45 camping tableware
46 camper
47 charcoal grill
(barbecue)
48 charcoal
49 bellows
50 roof rack
51 roof lashing
52 **caravan** (*Am.* trailer)
53 box for gas bottle
54 jockey wheel
55 drawbar coupling
56 roof ventilator
57 caravan awning
58 inflatable igloo tent
59 camp bed (*Am.* camp
cot)

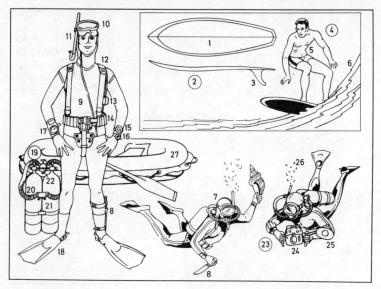

1–6 surf riding (surfing)
1 plan view of surfboard
2 section of surfboard
3 skeg (stabilizing fin)
4 big wave riding
5 surfboarder (surfer)
6 breaker
7–27 skin diving (underwater swimming)
7 skin diver (underwater swimmer)
8–22 underwater swimming set
8 knife
9 neoprene wetsuit
10 diving mask (face mask, mask), a pressure-equalizing mask
11 snorkel (schnorkel)
12 harness of diving apparatus
13 compressed-air pressure gauge (*Am.* gage)
14 weight belt
15 depth gauge (*Am.* gage)
16 waterproof watch for checking duration of dive
17 decometer for measuring stages of ascent
18 fin (flipper)

19 diving apparatus (*also:* aqualung, scuba), with two cylinders (bottles)
20 two-tube demand regulator
21 compressed-air cylinder (compressed-air bottle)
22 on/off valve
23 underwater photography
24 underwater camera
25 underwater flashlight
26 exhaust bubbles
27 inflatable boat (inflatable dinghy)

1 lifesaver (lifeguard)
2 lifeline
3 lifebelt (lifebuoy)
4 storm signal
5 time ball
6 warning sign
7 tide table, a notice board showing times of low tide and high tide
8 board showing water and air temperature
9 bathing platform
10 pennon staff
11 pennon
12 paddle boat (peddle boat)
13 surf riding (surfing) behind motorboat
14 surfboarder (surfer)
15 surfboard
16 water ski
17 inflatable beach mattress
18 beach ball
19–23 beachwear
19 beach suit
20 beach hat
21 beach jacket
22 beach trousers
23 beach shoe (bathing shoe)

24 beach bag
25 bathing gown (bathing wrap)
26 bikini (ladies' two–piece bathing suit)
27 bikini bottom
28 bikini top
29 bathing cap (swimming cap)
30 bather
31 deck tennis (quoits)
32 rubber ring (quoit)
33 inflatable rubber animal
34 beach attendant
35 sandcastle
36 roofed wicker beach chair
37 underwater swimmer
38 diving goggles
39 snorkel (schnorkel)
40 hand harpoon (fish spear, fish lance)
41 fin (flipper) for diving (for underwater swimming)
42 bathing suit (swimsuit)
43 bathing trunks (swimming trunks)
44 bathing cap (swimming cap)
45 beach tent, a ridge tent
46 lifeguard station

78 Swimming Bath (Leisure Centre, *Am.* Center)

1-9 swimming pool with artificial waves, an indoor pool
1 artificial waves
2 beach area
3 edge of the pool
4 swimming pool attendant (pool attendant, swimming bath attendant)
5 sun bed
6 lifebelt
7 water wings
8 bathing cap
9 channel to outdoor mineral bath
10 solarium
11 sunbathing area
12 sun bather
13 sun ray lamp
14 bathing towel
15 nudist sunbathing area
16 nudist (naturist)
17 screen (fence)
18 sauna (mixed sauna)
19 wood panelling (*Am.* paneling)
20 tiered benches
21 sauna stove
22 stones
23 hygrometer
24 thermometer
25 towel
26 water tub for moistening the stones in the stove
27 birch rods (birches) for beating the skin
28 cooling room for cooling off (cooling down) after the sauna
29 lukewarm shower
30 cold bath
31 hot whirlpool (underwater massage bath)
32 step into the bath
33 massage bath
34 jet blower
35 hot whirlpool [diagram]
36 section of the bath
37 step
38 circular seat
39 water extractor
40 water jet pipe
41 air jet pipe

79 Swimming

1-32 **swimming pool**, an open-air swimming pool
1 changing cubicle
2 shower (shower bath)
3 changing room
4 sunbathing area
5-10 **diving boards** (diving apparatus)
5 diver (highboard diver)
6 diving platform
7 ten-metre (*Am.* ten-meter) platform
8 five-metre (*Am.* five-meter) platform
9 three-metre (*Am.* three-meter) springboard (diving board)
10 one-metre (*Am.* one-meter) springboard
11 diving pool
12 straight header
13 feet-first jump
14 tuck jump (haunch jump)
15 swimming pool attendant (pool attendant, swimming bath attendant)
16-20 **swimming instruction**
16 swimming instructor (swimming teacher)
17 learner-swimmer
18 float; *sim.:* water wings
19 swimming belt (cork jacket)
20 land drill
21 non-swimmers' pool
22 footbath
23 swimmers' pool
24-32 **freestyle relay race**
24 timekeeper (lane timekeeper)
25 placing judge
26 turning judge
27 starting block (starting place)
28 competitor touching the finishing line
29 starting dive (racing dive)
30 starter
31 swimming lane
32 rope with cork floats
33-39 **swimming strokes**
33 breaststroke
34 butterfly stroke
35 dolphin butterfly stroke
36 side stroke

37 crawl stroke (crawl); *sim.:* trudgen stroke (trudgen, double overarm stroke)
38 underwater swimming
39 treading water
40-45 **diving** (acrobatic diving, fancy diving, competitive diving, highboard diving)
40 standing take-off pike dive
41 one-half twist isander (reverse dive)
42 backward somersault (double backward somersault)
43 running take-off twist dive
44 screw dive
45 armstand dive (handstand dive)
46-50 **water polo**
46 goal
47 goalkeeper
48 water polo ball
49 back
50 forward

80 Rowing and Canoeing

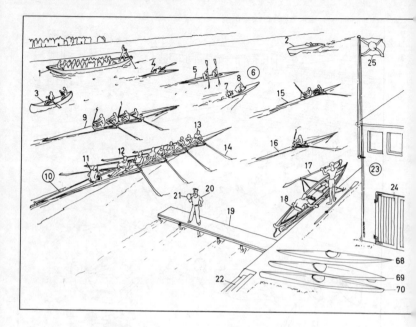

1-18 taking up positions for the
    regatta
1 punt, a pleasure boat
2 motorboat
3 Canadian canoe
4 kayak (Alaskan canoe, slalom
    canoe), a canoe
5 tandem kayak
6 outboard motorboat (outboard
    speedboat, outboard)
7 outboard motor (outboard)
8 cockpit
9-16 racing boats (sportsboats)
9-15 shells (rowing boats, *Am.*
    rowboats)
9 coxless four, a carvel-built boat
10 eight (eight-oared racing shell)
11 cox
12 stroke, an oarsman
13 bow ('number one')
14 oar
15 coxless pair
16 single sculler (single skuller,
    racing sculler, racing skuller,
    skiff)
17 scull (skull)
18 coxed single, a clinker-built
    single
19 jetty (landing stage, mooring)
20 rowing coach
21 megaphone
22 quayside steps
23 clubhouse (club)
24 boathouse
25 club's flag
26-33 four-oared gig, a touring boat
26 oar
27 cox's seat
28 thwart (seat)
29 rowlock (oarlock)
30 gunwale (gunnel)
31 rising
32 keel
33 skin (shell, outer skin) [clinker-
    built]
34 single-bladed paddle (paddle)
35-38 oar (scull, skull)
35 grip
36 leather sheath
37 shaft (neck)

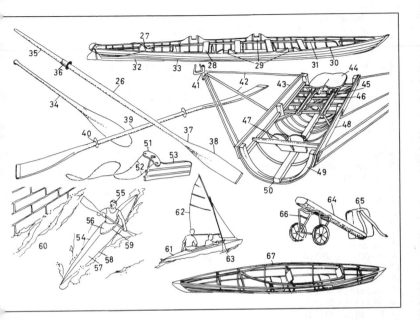

38 blade
39 double-bladed paddle (double-ended paddle)
40 drip ring
41–50 sliding seat
41 rowlock (oarlock)
42 outrigger
43 saxboard
44 sliding seat
45 runner
46 strut
47 stretcher
48 skin (shell, outer skin)
49 frame (rib)
50 kelson (keelson)
51–53 rudder (steering rudder)
51 yoke
52 lines (steering lines)
53 blade (rudder blade, rudder)
54–66 folding boats (foldboats, canoes)
54 one-man kayak
55 canoeist
56 spraydeck
57 deck

58 rubber-covered canvas hull
59 cockpit coaming (coaming)
60 channel for rafts alongside weir
61 two-seater folding kayak, a touring kayak
62 sail of folding kayak
63 leeboard
64 bag for the rods
65 rucksack
66 boat trailer (boat carriage)
67 frame of folding kayak
68–70 kayaks
68 Eskimo kayak
69 wild-water racing kayak
70 touring kayak

81 Sailing (Yachting) I

1–9 windsurfing
1 windsurfer
2 sail
3 transparent window (window)
4 mast
5 surfboard
6 universal joint (movable
   bearing) for adjusting the angle
   of the mast and for steering
7 boom
8 retractable centreboard (*Am.*
   centerboard)
9 rudder
10–48 yacht (sailing boat, *Am.*
   sailboat)
10 foredeck
11 mast
12 trapeze
13 crosstrees (spreader)
14 hound
15 forestay
16 jib (Genoa jib)
17 jib downhaul
18 side stay (shroud)
19 lanyard (bottlescrew)
20 foot of the mast
21 kicking strap (vang)
22 jam cleat
23 foresheet (jib sheet)
24 centreboard (*Am.* centerboard)
   case
25 bitt
26 centreboard (*Am.* centerboard)
27 traveller (*Am.* traveler)
28 mainsheet
29 fairlead
30 toestraps (hiking straps)
31 tiller extension (hiking stick)
32 tiller
33 rudderhead (rudder stock)
34 rudder blade (rudder)
35 transom
36 drain plug
37 gooseneck
38 window
39 boom
40 foot
41 clew
42 luff (leading edge)
43 leech pocket (batten cleat, batten
   pocket)
44 batten
45 leech (trailing edge)

46 mainsail
47 headboard
48 racing flag (burgee)
49–65 yacht classes
49 Flying Dutchman
50 O–Joller
51 Finn dinghy (Finn)
52 pirate
53 12.00 m² sharpie
54 tempest
55 star
56 soling
57 dragon
58 5.5–metre (*Am.* 5.5–meter) class
59 6–metre (*Am.* 6–meter) R–class
60 30.00 m² cruising yacht (coastal
   cruiser)
61 30.00 m² dinghy cruiser
62 25.00 m² one–design keelboat
63 KR–class
64 catamaran
65 twin hull

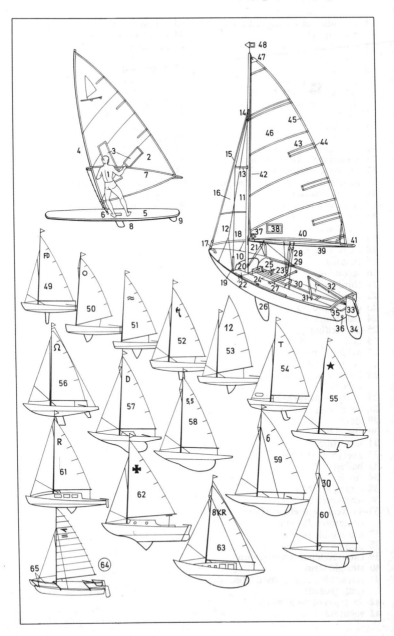

82 Sailing (Yachting) II

1-13 **points of sailing and wind directions**
1 sailing downwind
2 mainsail
3 jib
4 ballooning sails
5 centre (*Am.* center) line
6 wind direction
7 yacht tacking
8 sail, shivering
9 luffing
10 sailing close–hauled
11 sailing with wind abeam
12 sailing with free wind
13 quartering wind (quarter wind)
14-24 **regatta course**
14 starting and finishing buoy
15 committee boat
16 triangular course (regatta course)
17 buoy (mark) to be rounded
18 buoy to be passed
19 first leg
20 second leg
21 third leg
22 windward leg
23 downwind leg
24 reaching leg
25-28 **tacking**
25 tack
26 gybing (jibing)
27 going about
28 loss of distance during the gybe (jibe)
29-41 **types of yacht hull**
29-34 cruiser keelboat
29 stern
30 spoon bow
31 waterline
32 keel (ballast keel)
33 ballast
34 rudder
35 racing keelboat
36 lead keel
37-41 keel–centreboard (*Am.* centerboard) yawl
37 retractable rudder
38 cockpit
39 cabin superstructure (cabin)
40 straight stem
41 retractable centreboard (*Am.* centerboard)
42-49 **types of yacht stern**
42 yacht stern

43 square stern
44 canoe stern
45 cruiser stern
46 name plate
47 deadwood
48 transom stern
49 transom
50-57 **timber planking**
50-52 clinker planking (clench planking)
50 outside strake
51 frame (rib)
52 clenched nail (riveted nail)
53 carvel planking
54 close–seamed construction
55 stringer
56 diagonal carvel planking
57 inner planking

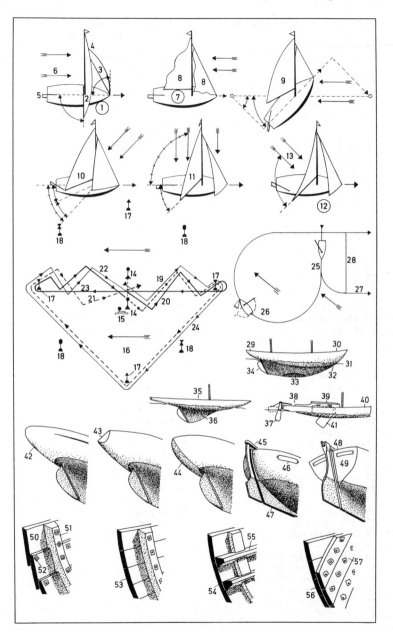

83 Motorboats (Powerboats), Water Skiing

1–5 motorboats (powerboats, sportsboats)
1 inflatable sportsboat with outboard motor (outboard inflatable)
2 Z–drive motorboat (outdrive motorboat)
3 cabin cruiser
4 motor cruiser
5 30–metre (*Am.* 30–meter) ocean-going cruiser
6 association flag
7 name of craft (*or:* registration number)
8 club membership and port of registry (*Am.* home port)
9 association flag on the starboard crosstrees
10–14 navigation lights of sportsboats in coastal and inshore waters
10 white top light
11 green starboard sidelight
12 red port sidelight
13 green and red bow light (combined lantern)
14 white stern light
15–18 anchors
15 stocked anchor (Admiralty anchor), a bower anchor
16–18 lightweight anchor
16 CQR anchor (plough, *Am.* plow, anchor)
17 stockless anchor (patent anchor)
18 Danforth anchor
19 life raft
20 life jacket
21–44 powerboat racing
21 catamaran with outboard motor
22 hydroplane
23 racing outboard motor
24 tiller
25 fuel pipe
26 transom
27 buoyancy tube
28 start and finish
29 start
30 starting and finishing line
31 buoy to be rounded
32–37 displacement boats
32–34 round–bilge boat
32 view of hull bottom
33 section of fore ship

34 section of aft ship
35–37 V–bottom boat (vee–bottom boat)
35 view of hull bottom
36 section of fore ship
37 section of aft ship
38–44 planing boats (surface skimmers, skimmers)
38–41 stepped hydroplane (stepped skimmer)
38 side view
39 view of hull bottom
40 section of fore ship
41 section of aft ship
42 three–point hydroplane
43 fin
44 float
45–62 water skiing
45 water skier
46 deep–water start
47 tow line (towing line)
48 handle
49–55 water–ski signalling (code of hand signals from skier to boat driver)
49 signal for 'faster'
50 signal for 'slower' ('slow down')
51 signal for 'speed OK'
52 signal for 'turn'
53 signal for 'stop'
54 signal for 'cut motor'
55 signal for 'return to jetty' ('back to dock')
56–62 types of water ski
56 trick ski (figure ski), a monoski
57–58 rubber binding
57 front foot binding
58 heel flap
59 strap support for second foot
60 slalom ski
61 skeg (fixed fin, fin)
62 jump ski
63 hovercraft (air–cushion vehicle)
64 propeller
65 rudder
66 skirt enclosing air cushion

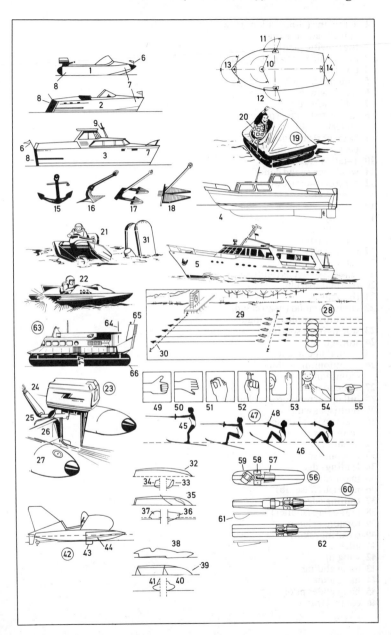

84 Gliding (Soaring)

1 aeroplane (*Am.* airplane) tow
   launch (aerotowing)
2 tug (towing plane)
3 towed glider (towed sailplane)
4 tow rope
5 winched launch
6 motor winch
7 cable parachute
8 motorized glider (powered
   glider)
9 high–performance glider (high–
   performance sailplane)
10 T–tail (T–tail unit)
11 wind sock (wind cone)
12 control tower (tower)
13 glider field
14 hangar
15 runway for aeroplanes (*Am.*
   airplanes)
16 wave soaring
17 lee waves (waves, wave system)
18 rotor
19 lenticular clouds (lenticulars)
20 thermal soaring
21 thermal
22 cumulus cloud (heap cloud,
   cumulus, woolpack cloud)
23 storm–front soaring
24 storm front
25 frontal upcurrent
26 cumulonimbus cloud
   (cumulonimbus)
27 slope soaring
28 hill upcurrent (orographic lift)
29 multispar wing
30 main spar, a box spar
31 connector fitting
32 anchor rib
33 diagonal spar
34 leading edge
35 main rib
36 nose rib (false rib)
37 trailing edge
38 brake flap (spoiler)
39 torsional clamp
40 covering (skin)
41 aileron
42 wing tip
43 hang gliding
44 hang glider
45 hang glider pilot
46 control frame

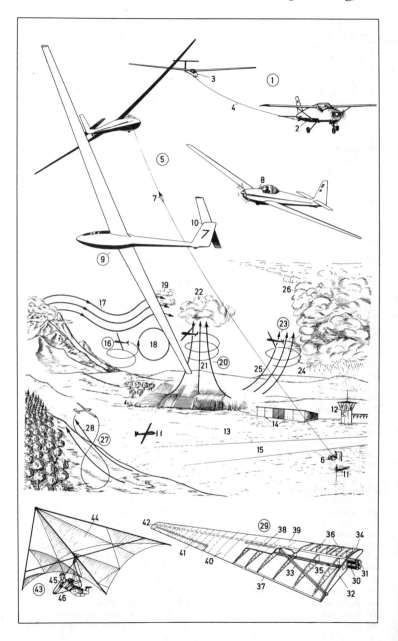

85 Aerial Sports (Airsports)

**1-9 aerobatics, aerobatic
manoeuvres** (*Am*. maneuvers)
1 loop
2 horizontal eight
3 rolling circle
4 stall turn (hammer head)
5 tail slide (whip stall)
6 vertical flick spin
7 spin
8 horizontal slow roll
9 inverted flight (negative flight)
10 **cockpit**
11 instrument panel
12 compass
13 radio and navigation equipment
14 control column (control stick)
15 throttle lever (throttle control)
16 mixture control
17 radio equipment
18 **two-seater plane for racing and
aerobatics**
19 cabin
20 antenna
21 vertical stabilizer (vertical fin,
tail fin)
22 rudder
23 tailplane (horizontal stabilizer)
24 elevator
25 trim tab (trimming tab)
26 fuselage (body)
27 wing
28 aileron
29 landing flap
30 trim tab (trimming tab)
31 navigation light (position light) [red]
32 landing light
33 main undercarriage unit (main
landing gear unit)
34 nose wheel
35 engine
36 propeller (airscrew)
37-62 parachuting
37 parachute
38 canopy
39 pilot chute
40 suspension lines
41 steering line
42 riser
43 harness
44 pack
45 system of slots of the sports
parachute
46 turn slots
47 apex

48 skirt
49 stabilizing panel
50-51 style jump
50 back loop
51 spiral
52-54 ground signals
52 signal for 'permission to jump'
('conditions are safe') (target cross)
53 signal for 'parachuting
suspended – repeat flight'
54 signal for 'parachuting
suspended – aircraft must land'
55 accuracy jump
56 target cross
57 inner circle [radius 25 m]
58 middle circle [radius 50 m]
59 outer circle [radius 100 m]
60-62 free-fall positions
60 full spread position
61 frog position
62 T position
63-84 ballooning
63 gas balloon
64 gondola (balloon basket)
65 ballast (sandbags)
66 mooring line
67 hoop
68 flight instruments (instruments)
69 trail rope
70 mouth (neck)
71 neck line
72 emergency rip panel
73 emergency ripping line
74 network (net)
75 rip panel
76 ripping line
77 valve
78 valve line
79 hot-air balloon
80 burner platform
81 mouth
82 vent
83 rip panel
84 balloon take-off
85-91 flying model aeroplanes (*Am*.
airplanes)
85 radio-controlled model flight
86 remote-controlled free flight
model
87 remote control radio
88 antenna (transmitting antenna)
89 control line model
90 mono-line control system
91 flying kennel, a K9-class model

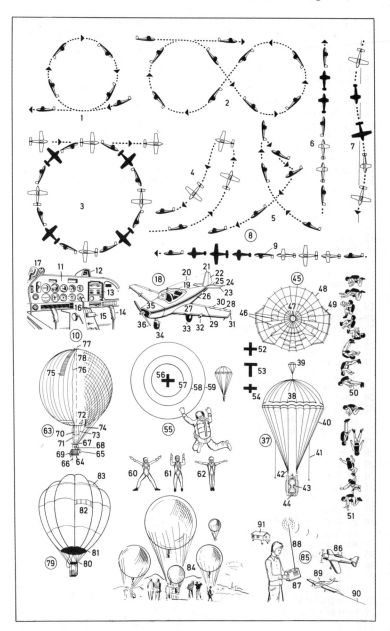

86 Horsemanship, Equestrian Sport

1-7 dressage
1 arena (dressage arena)
2 rail
3 school horse
4 dark coat (black coat)
5 white breeches
6 top hat
7 gait (*also:* school figure)
8-14 show jumping
8 obstacle (fence), an almost-fixed obstacle; *sim.:* gate, gate and rails, palisade, oxer, mound, wall
9 jumper
10 jumping saddle
11 girth
12 snaffle
13 red coat (hunting pink, pink; *also:* dark coat)
14 hunting cap (riding cap)
15 bandage
16-19 three-day event
16 endurance competition
17 cross-country
18 helmet (*also:* hard hat, hard hunting cap)
19 course markings
20-22 steeplechase
20 water jump, a fixed obstacle
21 jump
22 riding switch
23-40 harness racing (harness horse racing)
23 harness racing track (track)
24 sulky
25 spoke wheel (spoked wheel) with plastic wheel disc (disk)
26 driver in trotting silks
27 rein
28 trotter
29 piebald horse
30 shadow roll
31 elbow boot
32 rubber boot
33 number
34 glass-covered grandstand with totalizator windows (tote windows) inside
35 totalizator (tote)
36 number
37 odds (price, starting price, price offered)
38 winners' table
39 winner's price

40 time indicator
41-49 hunt, a drag hunt; *sim.:* fox hunt, paper chase (paper hunt, hare-and-hounds)
41 field
42 hunting pink
43 whipper-in (whip)
44 hunting horn
45 Master (Master of foxhounds, MFH)
46 pack of hounds (pack)
47 staghound
48 drag
49 scented trail (artificial scent)
50 horse racing (racing)
51 field (racehorses)
52 favourite (*Am.* favorite)
53 outsider

144

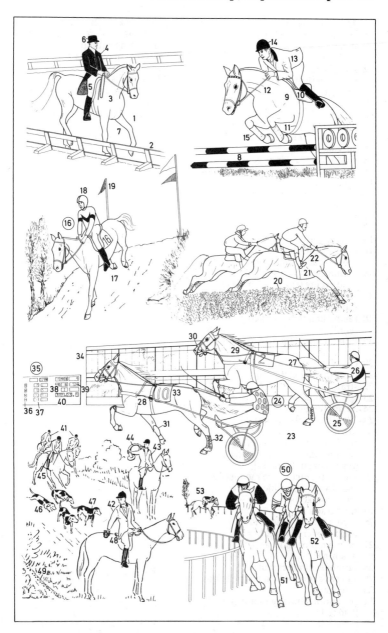

87 Cycle Racing and Motorsports

1-23 cycle racing
1 cycling track (cycle track); *here:* indoor track
2-7 six-day race
2 six-day racer, a track racer (track rider) on the track
3 crash hat
4 stewards
5 judge
6 lap scorer
7 rider's box (racer's box)
8-10 road race
8 road racer, a racing cyclist
9 racing jersey
10 water bottle
11-15 motor-paced racing (long-distance racing)
11 pacer, a motorcyclist
12 pacer's motorcycle
13 roller, a safety device
14 stayer (motor-paced track rider)
15 motor-paced cycle, a racing cycle
16 racing cycle (racing bicycle) for road racing (road race bicycle)
17 racing saddle, an unsprung saddle
18 racing handlebars (racing handlebar)
19 tubular tyre (*Am.* tire) (racing tyre)
20 chain
21 toe clip (racing toe clip)
22 strap
23 spare tubular tyre (*Am.* tire)
24-38 motorsports
24-28 motorcycle racing; *disciplines:* grasstrack racing, road racing, sand track racing, cement track racing, speedway [on ash or shale tracks], mountain racing, ice racing (ice speedway), scramble racing, trial, moto cross
24 sand track
25 racing motorcyclist (rider)
26 leather overalls (leathers)
27 racing motorcycle, a solo machine
28 number (number plate)
29 sidecar combination on the bend
30 sidecar
31 streamlined racing motorcycle [500 cc.]
32 gymkhana, a competition of skill; *here:* motorcyclist performing a jump
33 cross-country race, a test in performance
34-38 racing cars
34 Formula One racing car (a mono posto)
35 rear spoiler (aerofoil, *Am.* airfoil)
36 Formula Two racing car
37 Super-Vee racing car
38 prototype, a racing car

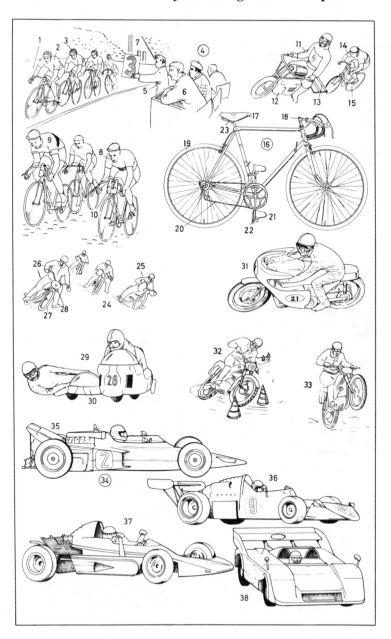

88 Ball Games I (Football, Association Football, Soccer)

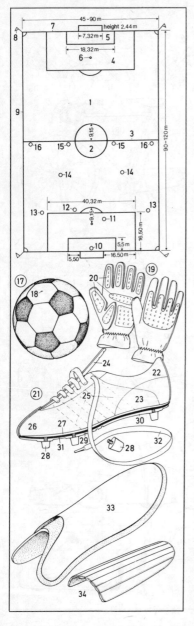

1–16 football pitch
1 field (park)
2 centre (*Am.* center) circle
3 half-way line
4 penalty area
5 goal area
6 penalty spot
7 goal line (by-line)
8 corner flag
9 touch line
10 goalkeeper
11 spare man
12 inside defender
13 outside defender
14 midfield players
15 inside forward (striker)
16 outside forward (winger)
17 football
18 valve
19 goalkeeper's gloves
20 foam rubber padding
21 football boot
22 leather lining
23 counter
24 foam rubber tongue
25 bands
26 shaft
27 insole
28 screw-in stud
29 groove
30 nylon sole
31 inner sole
32 lace (bootlace)
33 football pad with ankle guard
34 shin guard
35 goal
36 crossbar
37 post (goalpost)
38 goal kick
39 save with the fists
40 penalty (penalty kick)
41 corner (corner kick)
42 offside
43 free kick
44 wall
45 bicycle kick (overhead bicycle kick)
46 header
47 pass (passing the ball)
48 receiving the ball (taking a pass)
49 short pass (one-two)
50 foul (infringement)

148

51 obstruction
52 dribble
53 throw-in
54 substitute
55 coach
56 shirt (jersey)
57 shorts
58 sock (football sock)
59 linesman
60 linesman's flag
61 sending-off
62 referee
63 red card; *also:* yellow card
64 centre (*Am.* center) flag

89 Ball Games II

1 **handball** (indoor handball)
2 handball player, a field player
3 attacker, making a jump throw
4 defender
5 penalty line
6 **hockey**
7 goal
8 goalkeeper
9 pad (shin pad, knee pad)
10 kicker
11 face guard
12 glove
13 hockey stick
14 hockey ball
15 hockey player
16 striking circle
17 sideline
18 corner
19 **rugby** (rugby football)
20 scrum (scrummage)
21 rugby ball
22 **American football** (*Am.* football)
23 football player (player) carrying the ball
24 helmet
25 face guard
26 padded jersey
27 ball (pigskin)
28 **basketball**
29 basketball
30 backboard
31 basket posts
32 basket
33 basket ring
34 target rectangle
35 basketball player shooting
36 end line
37 restricted area
38 free-throw line
39 substitute
40–69 **baseball**
40–58 field (park)
40 spectator barrier
41 outfielder
42 short stop
43 second base
44 baseman
45 runner
46 first base
47 third base
48 foul line (base line)
49 pitcher's mound
50 pitcher

51 batter's position
52 batter
53 home base (home plate)
54 catcher
55 umpire
56 coach's box
57 coach
58 batting order
59–60 baseball gloves (baseball mitts)
59 fielder's glove (fielder's mitt)
60 catcher's glove (catcher's mitt)
61 baseball
62 bat
63 batter at bat
64 catcher
65 umpire
66 runner
67 base plate
68 pitcher
69 pitcher's mound
70–76 **cricket**
70 wicket with bails
71 back crease (bowling crease)
72 crease (batting crease)
73 wicket keeper of the fielding side
74 batsman
75 bat (cricket bat)
76 fielder (bowler)
77–82 **croquet**
77 winning peg
78 hoop
79 corner peg
80 croquet player
81 croquet mallet
82 croquet ball

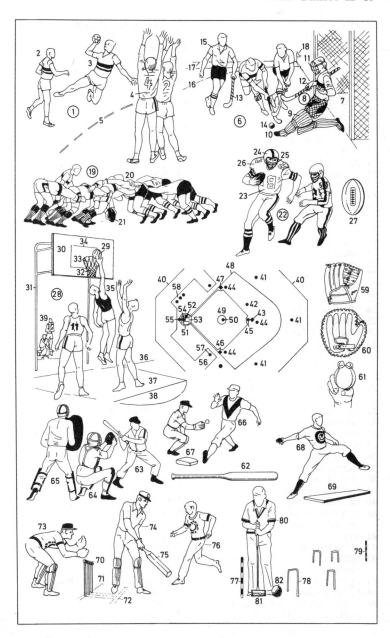

90 Ball Games III

1-42 tennis
1 tennis court
2 *to* 3 doubles sideline (sideline for doubles matches); *kinds of doubles:* men's doubles, women's doubles, mixed doubles
3 *to* 10 base line
4 *to* 5 singles sideline (sideline for singles matches); *kinds of singles:* men's singles, women's singles
6 *to* 7 service line
8 *to* 9 centre (*Am.* center) line
11 centre (*Am.* center) mark
12 service court
13 net (tennis net)
14 net strap
15 net post
16 tennis player
17 smash
18 opponent
19 umpire
20 umpire's chair
21 umpire's microphone
22 ball boy
23 net-cord judge
24 foot-fault judge
25 centre (*Am.* center) line judge
26 base line judge
27 service line judge
28 tennis ball
29 tennis racket (tennis racquet, racket, racquet)
30 racket handle (racquet handle)
31 strings (striking surface)
32 press (racket press, racquet press)
33 tightening screw
34 scoreboard
35 results of sets
36 player's name
37 number of sets
38 state of play
39 backhand stroke
40 forehand stroke
41 volley (forehand volley at normal height)
42 service

43-44 badminton
43 badminton racket (badminton racquet)
44 shuttle (shuttlecock)

45-55 table tennis
45 table tennis racket (racquet) (table tennis bat)

46 racket (racquet) handle (bat handle)
47 blade covering
48 table tennis ball
49 table tennis players; *here:* mixed doubles
50 receiver
51 server
52 table tennis table
53 table tennis net
54 centre (*Am.* center) line
55 sideline

56-71 volleyball
56-57 correct placing of the hands
58 volleyball
59 serving the volleyball
60 blocker
61 service area
62 server
63 front-line player
64 attack area
65 attack line
66 defence (*Am.* defense) area
67 referee
68 umpire
69 linesman
70 scoreboard
71 scorer

72-78 faustball
72 base line
73 tape
74 faust ball
75 forward
76 centre (*Am.* center)
77 back
78 hammer blow

79-93 golf
79-82 course (golf course, holes)
79 teeing ground
80 rough
81 bunker (*Am.* sand trap)
82 green (putting green)
83 golfer, driving
84 follow-through
85 golf trolley
86 putting (holing out)
87 hole
88 flagstick
89 golf ball
90 tee
91 wood, a driver; *sim.:* brassie (brassy, brassey)
92 iron
93 putter

91 Fencing

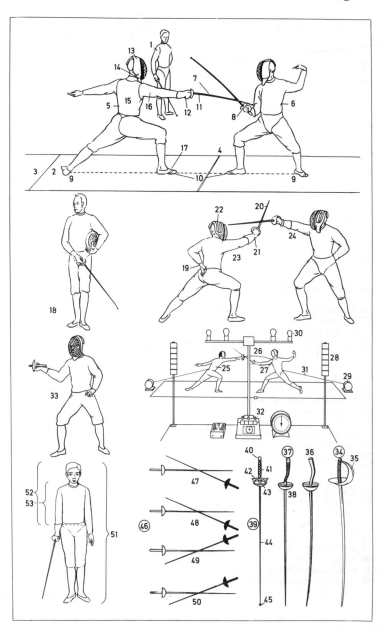

92 Free Exercise

1 basic position (starting position)
2 running posture
3 side straddle
4 straddle (forward straddle)
5 toe stand
6 crouch
7 upright kneeling position
8 kneeling position, seat on heels
9 squat
10 L seat (long sitting)
11 tailor seat (sitting tailor–style)
12 hurdle (hurdle position)
13 V–seat
14 side split
15 forward split
16 L–support
17 V–support
18 straddle seat
19 bridge
20 kneeling front support
21 front support
22 back support
23 crouch with front support
24 arched front support
25 side support
26 forearm stand (forearm balance)
27 handstand
28 headstand
29 shoulder stand (shoulder balance)
30 forward horizontal stand (arabesque)
31 rearward horizontal stand
32 trunk–bending sideways
33 trunk–bending forwards
34 arch
35 astride jump (butterfly)
36 tuck jump
37 astride jump
38 pike
39 scissor jump
40 stag jump (stag leap)
41 running step
42 lunge
43 forward pace
44 lying on back
45 prone position
46 lying on side
47 holding arms downwards
48 holding (extending) arms sideways
49 holding arms raised upward
50 holding (extending) arms forward
51 arms held (extended) backward
52 hands clasped behind the head

93 Apparatus Gymnastics I

1-11 gymnastics apparatus in men's Olympic gymnastics
1 long horse (horse, vaulting horse)
2 parallel bars
3 bar
4 rings (stationary rings)
5 pommel horse (side horse)
6 pommel
7 horizontal bar (high bar)
8 bar
9 upright
10 stay wires
11 floor (12 m x 12 m floor area)

12-21 auxiliary apparatus and apparatus for school and club gymnastics
12 springboard (Reuther board)
13 landing mat
14 bench
15 box
16 small box
17 buck
18 mattress
19 climbing rope (rope)
20 wall bars
21 window ladder

22-39 positions in relation to the apparatus
22 side, facing
23 side, facing away
24 end, facing
25 end, facing away
26 outside, facing
27 inside, facing
28 front support
29 back support
30 straddle position
31 seated position outside
32 riding seat outside
33 hang
34 reverse hang
35 hang with elbows bent
36 piked reverse hang
37 straight inverted hang
38 straight hang
39 bent hang

40-46 grasps (kinds of grasp)
40 overgrasp on the horizontal bar
41 undergrasp on the horizontal bar
42 combined grasp on the horizontal bar
43 cross grasp on the horizontal bar

44 rotated grasp on the horizontal bar
45 outside grip on the parallel bars
46 rotated grasp on the parallel bars
47 leather handstrap

48-60 exercises
48 long-fly on the horse
49 rise to straddle on the parallel bars
50 crucifix on the rings
51 scissors (scissors movement) on the pommel horse
52 legs raising into a handstand on the floor
53 squat vault on the horse
54 double leg circle on the pommel horse
55 hip circle backwards on the rings
56 lever hang on the rings
57 rearward swing on the parallel bars
58 forward kip into upper arm hang on the parallel bars
59 backward underswing on the horizontal bar
60 backward grand circle on the horizontal bar

61-63 gymnastics kit
61 singlet (vest, *Am.* undershirt)
62 gym trousers
63 gym shoes
64 wristband

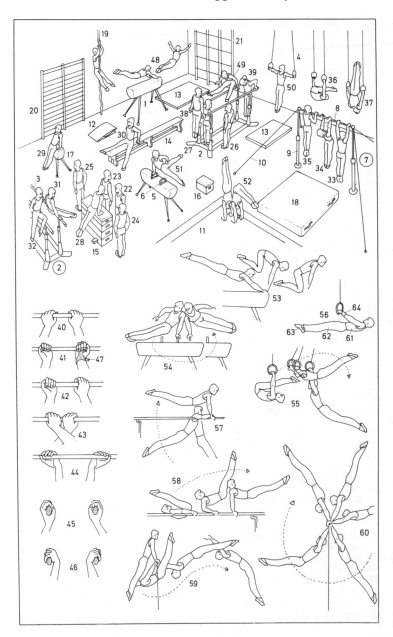

94 Apparatus Gymnastics II (Women's Gymnastics)

1–6 gymnastics apparatus in women's Olympic gymnastics
1 horse (vaulting horse)
2 beam
3 asymmetric bars (uneven bars)
4 bar
5 stay wires
6 floor (12 m x 12 m floor area)
7–14 auxiliary apparatus and apparatus for school and club gymnastics
7 landing mat
8 springboard (Reuther board)
9 small box
10 trampoline
11 sheet (web)
12 frame
13 rubber springs
14 springboard trampoline
15–32 apparatus exercises
15 backward somersault
16 spotting position (standing–in position)
17 vertical backward somersault on the trampoline
18 forward somersault on the springboard trampoline
19 forward roll on the floor
20 long–fly to forward roll on the floor
21 cartwheel on the beam
22 handspring on the horse
23 backward walkover
24 back flip (flik–flak) on the floor
25 free walkover forward on the floor
26 forward walkover on the floor
27 headspring on the floor
28 upstart on the asymmetric bars
29 free backward circle on the asymmetric bars
30 face vault over the horse
31 flank vault over the horse
32 back vault (rear vault) over the horse
33–50 gymnastics with hand apparatus
33 hand–to–hand throw
34 gymnastic ball
35 high toss
36 bounce
37 hand circling with two clubs
38 gymnastic club
39 swing
40 tuck jump
41 bar
42 skip
43 rope (skipping rope)
44 criss–cross skip
45 skip through the hoop
46 gymnastic hoop
47 hand circle
48 serpent
49 gymnastic ribbon
50 spiral
51–52 gymnastics kit
51 leotard
52 gym shoes

95 Athletics (Track and Field Events)

1-8 running
1-6 start
1 starting block
2 adjustable block (pedal)
3 start
4 crouch start
5 runner, a sprinter; *also:* middle-distance runner, long–distance runner
6 running track (track), a cinder track or synthetic track
7-8 hurdles (hurdle racing); *sim.:* steeplechase
7 clearing the hurdle
8 hurdle
9-41 jumping and vaulting
9-27 high jump
9 Fosbury flop (Fosbury, flop)
10 high jumper
11 body rotation (rotation on the body's longitudinal and latitudinal axes)
12 shoulder landing
13 upright
14 bar (crossbar)
15 Eastern roll
16 Western roll
17 roll
18 rotation
19 landing
20 height scale
21 Eastern cut–off
22 scissors (scissor jump)
23 straddle (straddle jump)
24 turn
25 vertical free leg
26 take–off
27 free leg
28-36 pole vault
28 pole (vaulting pole)
29 pole vaulter (vaulter) in the pull-up phase
30 swing
31 crossing the bar
32 high jump apparatus (high jump equipment)
33 upright
34 bar (crossbar)
35 box
36 landing area (landing pad)
37-41 long jump
37 take–off
38 take–off board

39 landing area
40 hitch–kick
41 hang
42-47 hammer throw
42 hammer
43 hammer head
44 handle
45 grip
46 holding the grip
47 glove
48 shot put
49 shot (weight)
50 O'Brien technique
51-53 javelin throw
51 grip with thumb and index finger
52 grip with thumb and middle finger
53 horseshoe grip
54 binding

96 Weightlifting and Combat Sports

1-5 weightlifting
1 squat–style snatch
2 weightlifter
3 disc (disk) barbell
4 jerk with split
5 maintained lift
6-12 wrestling
6-9 Greco-Roman wrestling
6 standing wrestling (wrestling in standing position)
7 wrestler
8 on–the–ground wrestling (*here:* the referee's position)
9 bridge
10-12 freestyle wrestling
10 bar arm (arm bar) with grapevine
11 double leg lock
12 wrestling mat (mat)
13-17 judo (*sim.:* ju-jitsu, jiu jitsu, ju-jutsu)
13 drawing the opponent off balance to the right and forward
14 judoka (judoist)
15 coloured (*Am.* colored) belt, as a symbol of Dan grade
16 referee
17 judo throw
18-19 karate
18 karateka
19 side thrust kick, a kicking technique
20-50 boxing (boxing match)
20-24 training apparatus (training equipment)
20 spring–supported punch ball
21 punch bag (*Am.* punching bag)
22 speed ball
23 suspended punch ball
24 punch ball
25 boxer, an amateur boxer (boxes in a singlet, vest, *Am.* undershirt) or a professional boxer (boxes without singlet)
26 boxing glove
27 sparring partner
28 straight punch (straight blow)
29 ducking and sidestepping
30 headguard
31 infighting; *here:* clinch
32 uppercut
33 hook to the head; *here:* right hook

34 punch below the belt, a foul punch (illegal punch, foul)
35-50 boxing match (boxing contest), a title fight (title bout)
35 boxing ring (ring)
36 ropes
37 stay wire (stay rope)
38 neutral corner
39 winner
40 loser by a knockout
41 referee
42 counting out
43 judge
44 second
45 manager
46 gong
47 timekeeper
48 record keeper
49 press photographer
50 sports reporter (reporter)

97 Mountaineering

1–57 **mountaineering** (mountain climbing, Alpinism)
1 hut (Alpine Club hut, mountain hut, base)
2–13 **climbing** (rock climbing) [rock climbing technique]
2 rock face (rock wall)
3 fissure (vertical, horizontal, or diagonal fissure)
4 ledge (rock ledge, grass ledge, scree ledge, snow ledge, ice ledge)
5 mountaineer (climber, mountain climber, Alpinist)
6 anorak (high–altitude anorak, snowshirt, padded jacket)
7 breeches (climbing breeches)
8 chimney
9 belay (spike, rock spike)
10 belay
11 rope sling (sling)
12 rope
13 spur
14–21 **snow and ice climbing** [snow and ice climbing technique]
14 ice slope (firn slope)
15 snow and ice climber
16 ice axe (*Am.* ax)
17 step (ice step)
18 snow goggles
19 hood (anorak hood)
20 cornice (snow cornice)
21 ridge (ice ridge)
22–27 **rope** (roped party)
22 glacier
23 crevasse
24 snow bridge
25 leader
26 second man (belayer)
27 third man (non–belayer)
28–30 **roping down** (abseiling, rapelling)
28 abseil sling
29 sling seat
30 Dülfer seat
31–57 **mountaineering equipment** (climbing equipment, snow and ice climbing equipment)
31 ice axe (*Am.* ax)
32 wrist sling
33 pick
34 adze (*Am.* adz)
35 karabiner hole

36 short–shafted ice axe (*Am.* ax)
37 hammer axe (*Am.* ax)
38 general–purpose piton
39 abseil piton (ringed piton)
40 ice piton (semi–tubular screw ice piton, corkscrew piton)
41 drive–in ice piton
42 mountaineering boot
43 corrugated sole
44 climbing boot
45 roughened stiff rubber upper
46 karabiner
47 screwgate
48 crampons (lightweight crampons, twelve–point crampons, ten–point crampons)
49 front points
50 point guards
51 crampon strap
52 crampon cable fastener
53 safety helmet (protective helmet)
54 helmet lamp
55 snow gaiters
56 climbing harness
57 sit harness

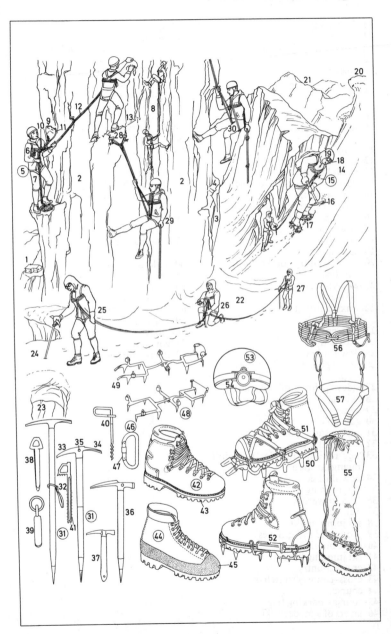

98 Winter Sports I (Skiing)

1–72 skiing
1 compact ski
2 safety binding (release binding)
3 strap
4 steel edge
5 ski stick (ski pole)
6 grip
7 loop
8 basket
9 ladies' one–piece ski suit
10 skiing cap (ski cap)
11 skiing goggles
12 cemented sole skiing boot
13 crash helmet
14–20 cross–country equipment
14 cross–country ski
15 cross–country rat trap binding
16 cross–country boot
17 cross–country gear
18 peaked cap
19 sunglasses
20 cross–country poles made of bamboo
21–24 ski–waxing equipment
21 ski wax
22 waxing iron (blowlamp, blowtorch)
23 waxing cork
24 wax scraper
25 downhill racing pole
26 herringbone, for climbing a slope
27 sidestep, for climbing a slope
28 ski bag
29 slalom
30 gate pole
31 racing suit
32 downhill racing
33 'egg' position, the ideal downhill racing position
34 downhill ski
35 ski jumping
36 lean forward
37 number
38 ski jumping ski
39 grooves (3 to 5 grooves)
40 cable binding
41 ski jumping boots
42 cross–country
43 cross–country stretch–suit
44 course
45 course–marking flag
46 layers of a modern ski

47 special core
48 laminates
49 stabilizing layer (stabilizer)
50 steel edge
51 aluminium (*Am.* aluminum) upper edge
52 synthetic bottom (artificial bottom)
53 safety jet
54–56 parts of the binding
54 automatic heel unit
55 toe unit
56 ski stop
57–63 ski lift
57 double chair lift
58 safety bar with footrest
59 ski lift
60 track
61 hook
62 automatic cable pulley
63 haulage cable
64 slalom
65 open gate
66 closed vertical gate
67 open vertical gate
68 transversal chicane
69 hairpin
70 elbow
71 corridor
72 Allais chicane

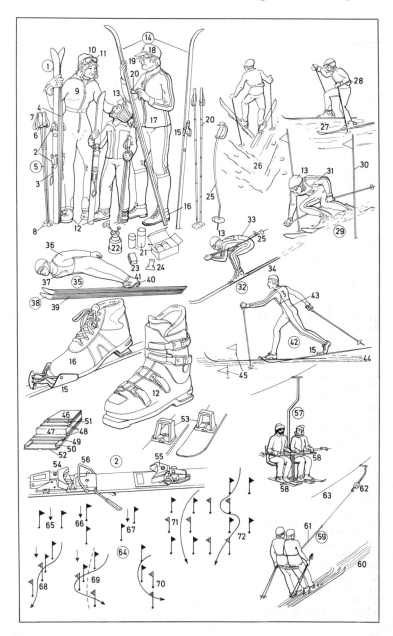

99 Winter Sports II

1–26 ice skating
1 ice skater, a solo skater
2 tracing leg
3 free leg
4 pair skaters
5 death spiral
6 pivot
7 stag jump (stag leap)
8 jump–sit–spin
9 upright spin
10 holding the foot
11–19 compulsory figures
11 curve eight
12 change
13 three
14 double–three
15 loop
16 change–loop
17 bracket
18 counter
19 rocker
20–25 ice skates
20 speed skating set (speed skate)
21 edge
22 hollow grinding (hollow ridge, concave ridge)
23 ice hockey set (ice hockey skate)
24 ice skating boot
25 skate guard
26 speed skater
27–28 skate sailing
27 skate sailor
28 hand sail
29–37 ice hockey
29 ice hockey player
30 ice hockey stick
31 stick handle
32 stick blade
33 shin pad
34 headgear (protective helmet)
35 puck, a vulcanized rubber disc (disk)
36 goalkeeper
37 goal
38–40 ice-stick shooting (Bavarian curling)
38 ice-stick shooter (Bavarian curler)
39 ice stick
40 block
41–43 curling
41 curler
42 curling stone (granite)

43 curling brush (curling broom, besom)
44–46 ice yachting (iceboating, ice sailing)
44 ice yacht (iceboat)
45 steering runner
46 outrigged runner

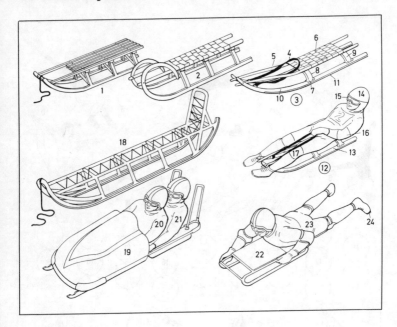

1 toboggan (sledge, *Am.* sled)
2 toboggan (sledge, *Am.* sled) with seat of plaid straps
3 junior luge toboggan (junior luge, junior toboggan)
4 rein
5 bar (strut)
6 seat
7 bracket
8 front prop
9 rear prop
10 movable runner
11 metal face
12 luge tobogganer
13 luge toboggan (luge, toboggan)
14 crash helmet
15 goggles
16 elbow pad
17 knee pad
18 Nansen sledge, a polar sledge
19-21 bobsleigh (bobsledding)
19 bobsleigh (bobsled), a two-man bobsleigh (a boblet)
20 steersman
21 brakeman

22-24 skeleton tobogganing (Cresta tobogganing)
22 skeleton (skeleton toboggan)
23 skeleton rider
24 rake, for braking and steering

1 avalanche (snow avalanche, *Am.* snowslide); *kinds:* wind avalanche, ground avalanche
2 avalanche wall, a deflecting wall (diverting wall); *sim.:* avalanche wedge
3 avalanche gallery
4 snowfall
5 snowdrift
6 snow fence
7 avalanche forest [planted as protection against avalanches]
8 street–cleaning lorry (street cleaner)
9 snow plough (*Am.* snowplow) attachment
10 snow chain (skid chain, tyre chain, *Am.* tire chain)
11 radiator bonnet (*Am.* radiator hood)
12 radiator shutter and shutter opening (louvre shutter)
13 snowman
14 snowball fight
15 snowball

16 ski bob
17 slide
18 boy, sliding
19 icy surface (icy ground)
20 snow–covered roof
21 icicle
22 man clearing snow
23 snow push (snow shovel)
24 heap of snow
25 horse-drawn sleigh (horse sleigh)
26 sleigh bells (bells, set of bells)
27 foot muff (*Am.* foot bag)
28 earmuff
29 handsledge (tread sledge); *sim.:* push sledge
30 slush

102 Various Sports

1-13 **skittles**
1-11 skittle frame
1 front pin (front)
2 left front second pin (left front second)
3 running three [left]
4 right front second pin (right front second)
5 running three [right]
6 left corner pin (left corner), a corner (copper)
7 landlord
8 right corner pin (right corner), a corner (copper)
9 back left second pin (back left second)
10 back right second pin (back right second)
11 back pin (back)
12 pin
13 landlord
14-20 **tenpin bowling**
14 frame
15 bowling ball (ball with finger holes)
16 finger hole
17-20 deliveries
17 straight ball
18 hook ball (hook)
19 curve
20 back-up ball (back-up)
21 boules; *sim.:* Italian game of boccie, green bowls (bowls)
22 boules player
23 jack (target jack)
24 grooved boule
25 group of players
26 **rifle shooting**
27-29 shooting positions
27 standing position
28 kneeling position
29 prone position
30-33 **targets**
30 target for 50 m events (50 m target)
31 circle
32 target for 100 m events (100 m target)
33 bobbing target (turning target, running-boar target)
34-39 **ammunition**
34 air rifle cartridge
35 rimfire cartridge for zimmerstutzen (indoor target rifle), a smallbore German single-shot rifle
36 case head
37 caseless round
38 .22 long rifle cartridge
39 .222 Remington cartridge
40-49 **sporting rifles**
40 air rifle
41 optical sight

42 front sight (foresight)
43 smallbore standard rifle
44 international smallbore free rifle
45 palm rest for standing position
46 butt plate with hook
47 butt with thumb hole
48 smallbore rifle for bobbing target (turning target)
49 telescopic sight (riflescope, telescope sight)
50 optical ring sight
51 optical ring and bead sight
52-66 **archery** (target archery)
52 shot
53 archer
54 competition bow
55 riser
56 point-of-aim mark
57 grip (handle)
58 stabilizer
59 bow string (string)
60 arrow
61 pile (point) of the arrow
62 fletching
63 nock
64 shaft
65 cresting
66 target
67 Basque game of pelota (jai alai)
68 pelota player
69 wicker basket (cesta)
70-78 **skeet** (skeet shooting), a kind of clay pigeon shooting
70 skeet over-and-under shotgun
71 muzzle with skeet choke
72 ready position on call
73 firing position
74 shooting range
75 high house
76 low house
77 target's path
78 shooting station (shooting box)
79 **aero wheel**
80 handle
81 footrest
82 **go-karting** (karting)
83 go-kart (kart)
84 number plate (number)
85 pedals
86 pneumatic tyre (*Am.* tire)
87 petrol tank (*Am.* gasoline tank)
88 frame
89 steering wheel
90 bucket seat
91 protective bulkhead
92 two-stroke engine
93 silencer (*Am.* muffler)

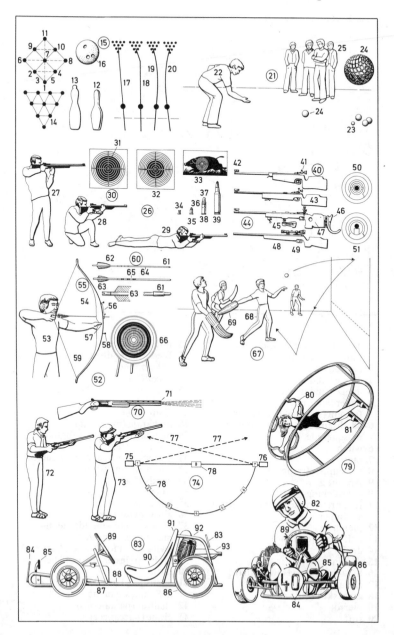

1–48 masked ball (masquerade, fancy-dress ball)
1 ballroom
2 dance band
3 dance band musician
4 paper lantern
5 festoon (string of decorations)
6–48 disguise (fancy dress) at the masquerade
6 witch
7 mask
8 fur trapper (trapper)
9 Apache girl
10 net stocking
11 first prize in the tombola (raffle), a hamper
12 pierette
13 half mask (domino)
14 devil
15 domino
16 hula-hula girl (Hawaii girl)
17 garland
18 grass skirt (hula skirt)
19 pierrot
20 ruff

21 midinette
22 Biedermeier dress
23 poke bonnet
24 décolletage with beauty spot
25 bayadère (Hindu dancing girl)
26 grandee
27 Columbine
28 maharaja (maharajah)
29 mandarin, a Chinese dignitary
30 exotic girl (exotic)
31 cowboy; *sim.:* gaucho (vaquero)
32 vamp, in fancy dress
33 dandy (fop)
34 rosette
35 harlequin
36 gipsy (gypsy) girl
37 cocotte (demi-monde, demi-mondaine, demi-rep)
38 owl-glass, a fool (jester, buffoon)
39 foolscap (jester's cap and bells)
40 rattle
41 odalisque, Eastern female slave in Sultan's seraglio
42 chalwar (pantaloons)
43 pirate (buccaneer)

44 tattoo
45 paper hat
46 false nose
47 clapper (rattle)
48 slapstick
49–54 fireworks
49 percussion cap
50 cracker
51 banger
52 jumping jack
53 cannon cracker (maroon,
   marroon)
54 rocket
55 paper ball
56 jack-in-the-box
57–70 carnival procession
57 carnival float (carnival truck)
58 King Carnival
59 bauble (fool's sceptre, *Am.*
   scepter)
60 fool's badge
61 Queen Carnival
62 confetti
63 giant
64 beauty queen

65 fairy-tale figure
66 paper streamer
67 majorette
68 king's guard
69 buffoon, a clown
70 lansquenet's drum

1-63 travelling (*Am.* traveling) circus
1 circus tent (big top), a four–pole tent
2 tent pole
3 spotlight
4 lighting technician
5 trapeze platform
6 trapeze
7 trapeze artist
8 rope ladder
9 bandstand
10 circus band
11 ring entrance (arena entrance)
12 wings
13 tent prop (prop)
14 safety net
15 seats for the spectators
16 circus box
17 circus manager
18 agent
19 entrance and exit
20 steps
21 ring (arena)
22 ring fence
23 musical clown (clown)
24 clown
25 comic turn (clown act), a circus act
26 circus riders (bareback riders)
27 ring attendant, a circus attendant
28 pyramid
29 support
30-31 performance by liberty horses
30 circus horse, performing the levade (pesade)
31 ringmaster
32 vaulter
33 emergency exit
34 caravan (circus caravan, *Am.* trailer)
35 springboard acrobat (springboard artist)
36 springboard
37 knife thrower
38 circus marksman
39 assistant
40 tightrope dancer
41 tightrope

42 balancing pole
43 throwing act
44 balancing act
45 support
46 pole (bamboo pole)
47 acrobat
48 equilibrist (balancer)
49 wild animal cage, a round cage
50 bars of the cage
51 passage (barred passage, passage
   for the wild animals)
52 tamer (wild animal tamer)
53 whip
54 fork
55 pedestal
56 wild animal (tiger, lion)
57 stand
58 hoop (jumping hoop)
59 seesaw
60 ball
61 camp
62 cage caravan
63 menagerie

105 Fair, Fairground

1-69 fair (annual fair)
1 fairground
2 children's merry-go-round, (whirligig), a roundabout (*Am.* carousel)
3 refreshment stall (drinks stall)
4 chairoplane
5 up-and-down roundabout
6 show booth (booth)
7 box (box office)
8 barker
9 medium
10 showman
11 try-your-strength machine
12 hawker
13 balloon
14 paper serpent
15 windmill
16 pickpocket (thief)
17 vendor
18 Turkish delight
19 freak show
20 giant
21 fat lady
22 dwarfs (midgets)

23 beer marquee
24 sideshow
25-28 travelling (*Am.* traveling) artistes (travelling show people)
25 fire eater
26 sword swallower
27 strong man
28 escapologist
29 spectators
30 ice-cream vendor (ice-cream man)
31 ice-cream cornet
32 hot-dog stand
33 grill (*Am.* broiler)
34 hot dog
35 sausage tongs
36 fortune teller
37 big wheel (Ferris wheel)
38 orchestrion (automatic organ)
39 scenic railway (switchback)
40 toboggan slide (chute)
41 swing boats
42 swing boat, turning full circle
43 full circle
44 lottery booth (tombola booth)

45 wheel of fortune
46 devil's wheel (typhoon wheel)
47 throwing ring (quoit)
48 prizes
49 sandwich man on stilts
50 sandwich board (placard)
51 cigarette seller, an itinerant
   trader (a hawker)
52 tray
53 fruit stall
54 wall–of–death rider
55 hall of mirrors
56 concave mirror
57 convex mirror
58 shooting gallery
59 hippodrome
60 junk stalls (second–hand stalls)
61 first aid tent (first aid post)
62 dodgems (bumper cars)
63 dodgem car (bumper car)

64–66 pottery stand
64 barker
65 market woman
66 pottery
67 visitors to the fair
68 waxworks
69 wax figure

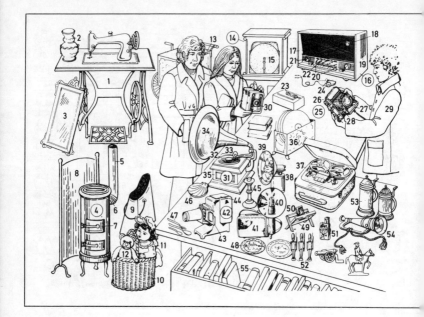

1 treadle sewing machine
2 flower vase
3 wall mirror
4 cylindrical stove
5 stovepipe
6 stovepipe elbow
7 stove door
8 stove screen
9 coal scuttle
10 firewood basket
11 doll
12 teddy bear
13 barrel organ
14 orchestrion
15 metal disc (disk)
16 radio (radio set, *joc.:* 'steam radio'), a superheterodyne (superhet)
17 baffle board
18 'magic eye', a tuning indicator valve
19 loudspeaker aperture
20 station selector buttons (station preset buttons)
21 tuning knob
22 frequency bands
23 crystal detector (crystal set)
24 headphones (headset)
25 folding camera
26 bellows
27 hinged cover
28 spring extension
29 salesman
30 box camera
31 gramophone
32 record (gramophone record)
33 needle head with gramophone needle
34 horn
35 gramophone box
36 record rack
37 portable tape recorder
38 flashgun
39 flash bulb
40–41 electronic flash (electronic flashgun)
40 flash head
41 accumulator
42 slide projector
43 slide holder

44 lamphouse
45 candlestick
46 scallop shell
47 cutlery
48 souvenir plate
49 drying rack for photographic plates
50 photographic plate
51 delayed-action release
52 tin soldiers (*sim.:* lead soldiers)
53 beer mug (stein)
54 bugle
55 second-hand books
56 grandfather clock
57 clock case
58 pendulum
59 time weight
60 striking weight
61 rocking chair
62 sailor suit
63 sailor's hat
64 washing set
65 washing basin
66 water jug
67 washstand

68 dolly
69 washtub
70 washboard
71 humming top
72 slate
73 pencil box
74 adding machine
75 paper roll
76 number keys
77 abacus
78 inkwell, with lid
79 typewriter
80 [hand-operated] calculating machine (calculator)
81 operating handle
82 result register (product register)
83 rotary counting mechanism (rotary counter)
84 kitchen scales
85 waist slip (underskirt)
86 wooden handcart
87 wall clock
88 bed warmer
89 milk churn

107 Films (Motion Pictures) I

1–13 film studios (studio complex,
  Am. movie studios)
1 lot (studio lot)
2 processing laboratories (film
  laboratories, motion picture
  laboratories)
3 cutting rooms
4 administration building (office
  building, offices)
5 film (motion picture) storage
  vault (film library, motion
  picture library)
6 workshop
7 film set (*Am.* movie set)
8 power house
9 technical and research
  laboratories
10 groups of stages
11 concrete tank for marine
  sequences
12 cyclorama
13 hill
14–60 shooting (filming)
14 music recording studio (music
  recording theatre, *Am.* theater)
15 'acoustic' wall lining

16 screen (projection screen)
17 film orchestra
18 exterior shooting (outdoor
  shooting, exterior filming,
  outdoor filming)
19 camera with crystal–controlled
  drive
20 cameraman
21 assistant director
22 boom operator (boom swinger)
23 recording engineer (sound
  recordist)
24 portable sound recorder with
  crystal–controlled drive
25 microphone boom
26–60 shooting (filming) in the
  studio (on the sound stage, on
  the stage, in the filming hall)
26 production manager
27 leading lady (film actress, film
  star, star)
28 leading man (film actor, film
  star, star)
29 film extra (extra)
30 arrangement of microphones for
  stereo and sound effects

184

31 studio microphone
32 microphone cable
33 side flats and background
34 clapper boy
35 clapper board (clapper) with slates (boards) for the film title, shot number (scene number), and take number
36 make–up artist (hairstylist)
37 lighting electrician (studio electrician, lighting man, *Am.* gaffer)
38 diffusing screen
39 continuity girl (script girl)
40 film director (director)
41 cameraman (first cameraman)
42 camera operator, an assistant cameraman (camera assistant)
43 set designer (art director)
44 director of photography
45 filmscript (script, shooting script, *Am.* movie script)
46 assistant director
47 soundproof film camera (soundproof motion picture camera), a wide screen camera (cinemascope camera)

48 soundproof housing (soundproof cover, blimp)
49 camera crane (dolly)
50 hydraulic stand
51 mask (screen) for protection from spill light (gobo, nigger)
52 tripod spotlight (fill–in light, filler light, fill light, filler)
53 spotlight catwalk
54 recording room
55 recording engineer (sound recordist)
56 mixing console (mixing desk)
57 sound assistant (assistant sound engineer)
58 magnetic sound recording equipment (magnetic sound recorder)
59 amplifier and special effects equipment, e.g. for echo and sound effects
60 sound recording camera (optical sound recorder)

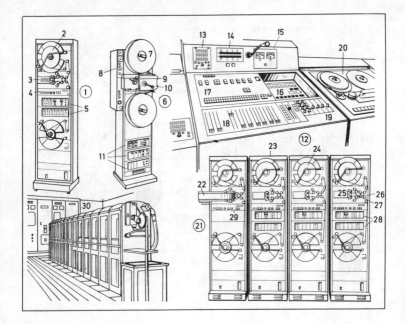

1–46 sound recording and re-recording (dubbing)
1 magnetic sound recording equipment (magnetic sound recorder)
2 magnetic film spool
3 magnetic head support assembly
4 control panel
5 magnetic sound recording and playback amplifier
6 optical sound recorder (sound recording camera, optical sound recording equipment)
7 daylight film magazine
8 control and monitoring panel
9 eyepiece for visual control of optical sound recording
10 deck
11 recording amplifier and mains power unit
12 control desk (control console)
13 monitoring loudspeaker (control loudspeaker)
14 recording level indicators
15 monitoring instruments

16 jack panel
17 control panel
18 sliding control
19 equalizer
20 magnetic sound deck
21 mixer for magnetic film
22 film projector
23 recording and playback equipment
24 film reel (film spool)
25 head support assembly for the recording head, playback head, and erasing head (erase head)
26 film transport mechanism
27 synchronizing filter
28 magnetic sound amplifier
29 control panel
30 film–processing machines (film–developing machines) in the processing laboratory (film laboratory, motion picture laboratory)
31 echo chamber
32 echo chamber loudspeaker
33 echo chamber microphone

34–36 sound mixing (sound dubbing, mixing of several sound tracks)
34 mixing room (dubbing room)
35 mixing console (mixing desk) for mono or stereo sound
36 dubbing mixers (recording engineers, sound recordists) dubbing (mixing)
37–41 synchronization (syncing, dubbing, post–synchronization, post–syncing)
37 dubbing studio (dubbing theatre, *Am.* theater)
38 dubbing director
39 dubbing speaker (dubbing actress)
40 boom microphone
41 microphone cable

42–46 cutting (editing)
42 cutting table (editing table, cutting bench)
43 film editor (cutter)
44 film turntable, for picture and sound tracks
45 projection of the picture
46 loudspeaker

1–23 film projection (motion
picture projection)
1 cinema (picture house, *Am*.
movie theater, movie house)
2 cinema box office (*Am*. movie
theater box office)
3 cinema ticket (*Am*. movie
theater ticket)
4 usherette
5 cinemagoers (filmgoers, cinema
audience, *Am*. moviegoers,
movie audience)
6 safety lighting (emergency
lighting)
7 emergency exit
8 stage
9 rows of seats (rows)
10 stage curtain (screen curtain)
11 screen (projection screen)
12 projection room (projection
booth)
13 lefthand projector
14 righthand projector
15 projection room window with
projection window and
observation port
16 reel drum (spool box)
17 house light dimmers
(auditorium lighting control)
18 rectifier, a selenium or mercury
vapour rectifier for the
projection lamps
19 amplifier
20 projectionist
21 rewind bench for rewinding the
film
22 film cement (splicing cement)
23 slide projector for
advertisements
24–52 film projectors
24 sound projector (film projector,
cinema projector, theatre
projector, *Am*. movie projector)
25–38 projector mechanism
25 fireproof reel drums (spool
boxes) with circulating oil
cooling system
26 feed sprocket (supply sprocket)
27 take–up sprocket
28 magnetic head cluster
29 guide roller (guiding roller) with
framing control

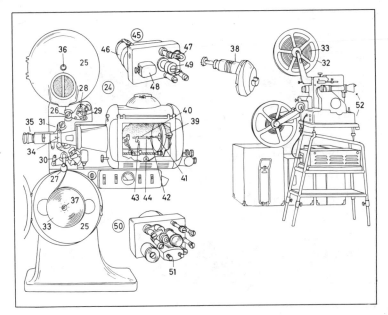

30 loop former for smoothing out the intermittent movement; *also:* film break detector
31 film path
32 film reel (film spool)
33 reel of film
34 film gate (picture gate, projector gate) with cooling fan
35 projection lens (projector lens)
36 feed spindle
37 take-up spindle with friction drive
38 maltese cross mechanism (maltese cross movement, Geneva movement)
39-44 lamphouse
39 mirror arc lamp, with aspherical (non-spherical) concave mirror and blowout magnet for stabilizing the arc (*also:* high-pressure xenon arc lamp)
40 positive carbon (positive carbon rod)
41 negative carbon (negative carbon rod)
42 arc

43 carbon rod holder
44 crater (carbon crater)
45 optical sound unit [also designed for multi-channel optical stereophonic sound and for push-pull sound tracks]
46 sound optics
47 sound head
48 exciter lamp in housing
49 photocell in hollow drum
50 attachable four-track magnetic sound unit (penthouse head, magnetic sound head)
51 four-track magnetic head
52 narrow-gauge (*Am.* narrow-gage) cinema projector for mobile cinema

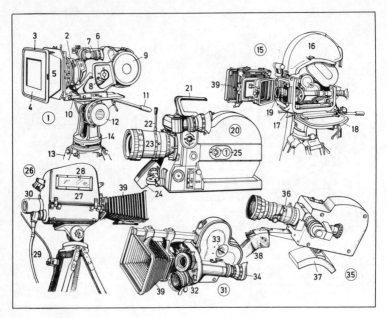

1-39 **motion picture cameras** (film cameras)
1 standard-gauge (*Am.* standard-gage) motion picture camera (standard-gauge, *Am.* standard-gage, 35 mm camera)
2 lens (object lens, taking lens)
3 lens hood (sunshade) with matte box
4 matte (mask)
5 lens hood barrel
6 viewfinder eyepiece
7 eyepiece control ring
8 opening control for the segment disc (disk) shutter
9 magazine housing
10 slide bar for the lens hood
11 control arm (control lever)
12 pan and tilt head
13 wooden tripod
14 degree scale
15 soundproof (blimped) motion picture camera (film camera)
16-18 soundproof housing (blimp)
16 upper section of the soundproof housing
17 lower section of the soundproof housing
18 open sidewall of the soundproof housing
19 camera lens

20 lightweight professional motion picture camera
21 grip (handgrip)
22 zooming lever
23 zoom lens (variable focus lens, varifocal lens) with infinitely variable focus
24 handgrip with shutter release
25 camera door
26 sound camera (newsreel camera) for recording sound and picture
27 soundproof housing (blimp)
28 window for the frame counters and indicator scales
29 pilot tone cable (sync pulse cable)
30 pilot tone generator (signal generator, pulse generator)
31 professional narrow-gauge (*Am.* narrow-gage) motion picture camera, a 16 mm camera
32 lens turret (turret head)
33 housing lock
34 eyecup
35 high-speed camera, a special narrow-gauge (*Am.* narrow-gage) camera
36 zooming lever
37 rifle grip
38 handgrip with shutter release
39 lens hood bellows

1–6 the five positions (ballet positions)
1 first position
2 second position
3 third position
4 fourth position [open]
5 fourth position [crossed; extended fifth position]
6 fifth position
7–10 ports de bras (arm positions)
7 port de bras à coté
8 port de bras en bas
9 port de bras en avant
10 port de bras en haut
11 dégagé à la quatrième devant
12 dégagé à la quatrième derrière
13 effacé
14 sur le cou-de-pied
15 écarté
16 croisé
17 attitude
18 arabesque
19 à pointe (on full point)
20 splits
21 cabriole (capriole)
22 entrechat (entrechat quatre)

23 préparation [e.g. for a pirouette]
24 pirouette
25 corps de ballet
26 ballet dancer (ballerina)
27–28 pas de trois
27 prima ballerina
28 principal male dancer (leading soloist)
29 tutu
30 point shoe, a ballet shoe (ballet slipper)
31 ballet skirt

1–4 types of curtain operation
1 draw curtain (side parting)
2 tableau curtain (bunching up sideways)
3 fly curtain (vertical ascent)
4 combined fly and draw curtain
5–11 cloakroom hall (*Am*. checkroom hall)
5 cloakroom (*Am*. checkroom)
6 cloakroom attendant (*Am*. checkroom attendant)
7 cloakroom ticket (*Am*. check)
8 playgoer (theatregoer, *Am*. theatergoer)
9 opera glass (opera glasses)
10 commissionaire
11 theatre (*Am*. theater) ticket, an admission ticket
12–13 foyer (lobby, crush room)
12 usher; *form.*: box attendant
13 programme (*Am*. program)
14–27 auditorium and stage
14 stage
15 proscenium
16–20 auditorium
16 gallery (balcony)
17 upper circle
18 dress circle (*Am*. balcony, mezzanine)
19 front stalls
20 seat (theatre seat, *Am*. theater seat)
21–27 rehearsal (stage rehearsal)
21 chorus
22 singer
23 singer
24 orchestra pit
25 orchestra
26 conductor
27 baton (conductor's baton)
28–42 paint room, a workshop
28 stagehand (scene shifter)
29 catwalk (bridge)
30 set piece
31 reinforcing struts
32 built piece (built unit)
33 backcloth (backdrop)
34 portable box for paint containers
35 scene painter
36 paint trolley
37 stage designer (set designer)
38 costume designer
39 design for a costume

40 sketch for a costume
41 model stage
42 model of the set
43–52 dressing room
43 dressing room mirror
44 make-up gown
45 make-up table
46 greasepaint stick
47 chief make-up artist (chief make-up man)
48 make-up artist (hairstylist)
49 wig
50 props (properties)
51 theatrical costume
52 call light

113 Theatre (*Am*. Theater) II

1–60 stagehouse with machinery
(machinery in the flies and
below stage)
1 control room
2 control console (lighting console,
lighting control console) with
preset control for presetting
lighting effects
3 lighting plot (light plot)
4 grid (gridiron)
5 fly floor (fly gallery)
6 sprinkler system for fire
prevention (for fire protection)
7 fly man
8 fly lines (lines)
9 cyclorama
10 backcloth (backdrop,
background)
11 arch, a drop cloth
12 border
13 compartment (compartment-
type, compartmentalized) batten
(*Am*. border light)
14 stage lighting units (stage lights)
15 horizon lights (backdrop lights)
16 adjustable acting area lights
(acting area spotlights)
17 scenery projectors (projectors)
18 monitor (water cannon) (a piece
of safety equipment)
19 travelling (*Am*. traveling)
lighting bridge (travelling
lighting gallery)
20 lighting operator (lighting man)
21 portal spotlight (tower spotlight)
22 adjustable proscenium
23 curtain (theatrical curtain)
24 iron curtain (safety curtain, fire
curtain)
25 forestage (apron)
26 footlight (footlights, floats)
27 prompt box
28 prompter
29 stage manager's desk
30 stage director (stage manager)
31 revolving stage
32 trap opening
33 lift (*Am*. elevator)
34 bridge (*Am*. elevator), a rostrum
35 pieces of scenery
36 scene
37 actor
38 actress

39 extras (supers, supernumeraries)
40 director (producer)
41 prompt book (prompt script)
42 director's table (producer's table)
43 assistant director (assistant
producer)
44 director's script (producer's
script)
45 stage carpenter
46 stagehand (scene shifter)
47 set piece
48 mirror spot (mirror spotlight)
49 automatic filter change (with
colour filters, colour mediums,
gelatines)
50 hydraulic plant room
51 water tank
52 suction pipe
53 hydraulic pump
54 pressure pipe
55 pressure tank (accumulator)
56 pressure gauge (*Am*. gage)
57 level indicator (liquid level
indicator)
58 control lever
59 operator
60 rams

114 Discotheque

1 bar
2 barmaid
3 bar stool
4 shelf for bottles
5 shelf for glasses
6 beer glass
7 wine and liqueur glasses
8 beer tap (tap)
9 bar
10 refrigerator (fridge, *Am.* icebox)
11 bar lamps
12 indirect lighting
13 colour (*Am.* color) organ (clavilux)
14 dance floor lighting
15 speaker (loudspeaker)
16 dance floor
17–18 dancing couple
17 dancer
18 dancer
19 record player
20 microphone
21 tape recorder

22–23 stereo system (stereo equipment)
22 tuner
23 amplifier
24 records (discs)
25 disc jockey
26 mixing console (mixing desk, mixer)
27 tambourine
28 mirrored wall
29 ceiling tiles
30 ventilators
31 toilets (lavatories, WC)
32 long drink
33 cocktail (*Am.* highball)

1–33 nightclub (night spot)
1 cloakroom (*Am.* checkroom)
2 cloakroom attendant (*Am.* checkroom attendant)
3 band
4 clarinet
5 clarinettist (*Am.* clarinetist)
6 trumpet
7 trumpeter
8 guitar
9 guitarist (guitar player)
10 drums
11 drummer
12 speaker (loudspeaker)
13 bar
14 barmaid
15 bar
16 bar stool
17 tape recorder
18 receiver
19 spirits
20 cine projector for porno films (sex films, blue movies)
21 box containing screen
22 stage

23 stage lighting
24 spotlight
25 festoon lighting
26 festoon lamp (lamp, light bulb)
27–32 striptease act (striptease number)
27 striptease artist (stripper)
28 suspender (*Am.* garter)
29 brassière (bra)
30 fur stole
31 gloves
32 stocking
33 hostess

116 Bullfighting, Rodeo

1–33 bullfight (corrida, corrida de toros)
1 mock bullfight
2 novillero
3 mock bull (dummy bull)
4 novice banderillero (apprentice banderillero)
5 bullring (plaza de toros) [diagram]
6 main entrance
7 boxes
8 stands
9 arena (ring)
10 bullfighters' entrance
11 torril door
12 exit gate for killed bulls
13 slaughterhouse
14 bull pens (corrals)
15 paddock
16 lancer on horseback (picador)
17 lance (pike pole, javelin)
18 armoured (*Am.* armored) horse
19 leg armour (*Am.* armor)
20 picador's round hat
21 banderillero, a torero
22 banderillas (barbed darts)
23 shirtwaist
24 bullfight
25 matador (swordsman), a torero
26 queue, a distinguishing mark of the matador
27 red cloak (capa)
28 fighting bull
29 montera [hat made of tiny black silk chenille balls]
30 killing the bull (kill)
31 matador in charity performances [without professional uniform]
32 estoque (sword)
33 muleta
34 rodeo
35 young bull
36 cowboy
37 stetson (stetson hat)
38 scarf (necktie)
39 rodeo rider
40 lasso

1 cashier
2 electric cash register (till)
3 number keys
4 cancellation button
5 cash drawer (till)
6 compartments (money compartments) for coins and notes (*Am.* bills)
7 receipt (sales check)
8 cash total
9 adding mechanism
10 goods
11 glass-roofed well
12 men's wear department
13 showcase (display case, indoor display window)
14 wrapping counter
15 tray for purchases
16 customer
17 hosiery department
18 shop assistant (*Am.* salesgirl, saleslady)
19 price card
20 glove stand

21 duffle coat, a three-quarter length coat
22 escalator
23 fluorescent light (fluorescent lamp)
24 office (e.g. customer accounts office, travel agency, manager's office)
25 poster (advertisement)
26 theatre (*Am.* theater) and concert booking office (advance booking office)
27 shelves
28 ladies' wear department
29 ready-made dress (ready-to-wear dress, *coll.* off-the-peg dress)
30 dust cover
31 clothes rack
32 changing booth (fitting booth)
33 shop walker (*Am.* floorwalker, floor manager)
34 dummy
35 seat (chair)

36 fashion journal (fashion magazine)
37 tailor marking a hemline
38 measuring tape (tape measure)
39 tailor's chalk (French chalk)
40 hemline marker
41 loose-fitting coat
42 sales counter
43 warm-air curtain
44 doorman (commissionaire)
45 lift (*Am.* elevator)
46 lift cage (lift car, *Am.* elevator car)
47 lift operator (*Am.* elevator operator)
48 controls (lift controls, *Am.* elevator controls)
49 floor indicator
50 sliding door
51 lift shaft (*Am.* elevator shaft)
52 bearer cable
53 control cable
54 guide rail
55 customer

56 hosiery
57 linen goods (table linen and bed linen)
58 fabric department
59 roll of fabric (roll of material, roll of cloth)
60 head of department (department manager)
61 sales counter
62 jewellery (*Am.* jewelry) department
63 assistant (*Am.* salesgirl, saleslady), selling new lines (new products)
64 special counter (extra counter)
65 placard advertising special offers
66 curtain department
67 display on top of the shelves

118 Park

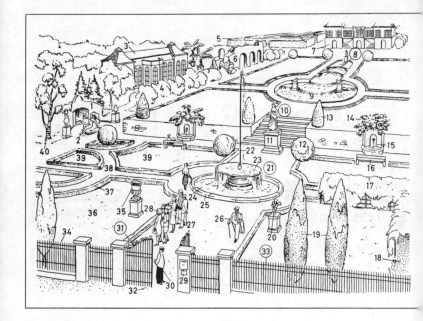

1–40 formal garden (French
Baroque garden), palace gardens
1 grotto (cavern)
2 stone statue, a river nymph
3 orangery (orangerie)
4 boscage (boskage)
5 maze (labyrinth of paths and
hedges)
6 open-air theatre (*Am.* theater)
7 Baroque palace
8 fountains
9 cascade (broken artificial
waterfall, artificial falls)
10 statue, a monument
11 pedestal (base of statue)
12 globe-shaped tree
13 conical tree
14 ornamental shrub
15 wall fountain
16 park bench
17 pergola (bower, arbour, *Am.*
arbor)
18 gravel path (gravel walk)
19 pyramid tree (pyramidal tree)
20 cupid (cherub, amoretto,
amorino)
21 fountain
22 fountain
23 overflow basin
24 basin
25 kerb (curb)
26 man out for a walk
27 tourist guide
28 group of tourists
29 park by-laws (bye-laws)
30 park keeper
31 garden gates, wrought iron gates
32 park entrance
33 park railings
34 railing (bar)
35 stone vase
36 lawn
37 border, a trimmed (clipped)
hedge
38 park path
39 parterre
40 birch (birch tree)

202

41–72 landscaped park (jardin anglais)
41 flower bed
42 park bench (garden seat)
43 litter bin (*Am.* litter basket)
44 play area
45 stream
46 jetty
47 bridge
48 park chair
49 animal enclosure
50 pond
51–54 waterfowl
51 wild duck with young
52 goose
53 flamingo
54 swan
55 island
56 water lily
57 open-air café
58 sunshade
59 tree
60 treetop (crown)
61 group of trees
62 fountain
63 weeping willow
64 modern sculpture
65 hothouse
66 park gardener
67 broom
68 minigolf course
69 minigolf player
70 minigolf hole
71 mother with pram (baby carriage)
72 courting couple (young couple)

1 table tennis
2 table
3 table tennis net
4 table tennis racket (raquet) (table tennis bat)
5 table tennis ball
6 badminton game (shuttlecock game)
7 shuttlecock
8 maypole swing
9 child's bicycle
10 football (soccer)
11 goal (goalposts)
12 football
13 goal scorer
14 goalkeeper
15 skipping (Am. jumping rope)
16 skipping rope (Am. skip rope, jump rope, jumping rope)
17 climbing tower
18 rubber tyre (Am. tire) swing
19 lorry tyre (Am. truck tire)
20 bouncing ball
21 adventure playground
22 log ladder

23 lookout platform
24 slide
25 litter bin (Am. litter basket)
26 teddy bear
27 wooden train set
28 paddling pool
29 sailing boat (yacht, Am. sailboat)
30 toy duck
31 pram (baby carriage)
32 high bar (bar)
33 go-cart (soap box)
34 starter's flag
35 seesaw
36 robot
37 flying model aeroplanes (Am. airplanes)
38 model aeroplane (Am. airplane)
39 double swing
40 swing seat
41 flying kites
42 kite
43 tail of the kite
44 kite string
45 revolving drum
46 spider's web

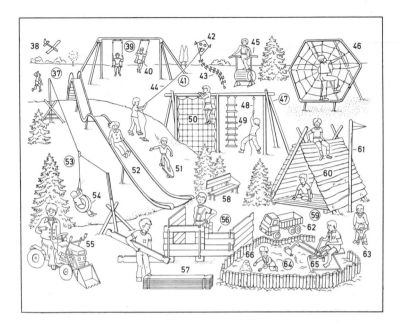

47 climbing frame
48 climbing rope
49 rope ladder
50 climbing net
51 skateboard
52 up-and-down slide
53 rubber tyre (*Am.* tire) cable car
54 rubber tyre (*Am.* tire)
55 tractor, a pedal car
56 den
57 presawn boards
58 seat (bench)
59 Indian hut
60 climbing roof
61 flagpole (flagstaff)
62 toy lorry (*Am.* toy truck)
63 walking doll
64 sandpit (*Am.* sandbox)
65 toy excavator (toy digger)
66 sandhill

1–21 spa gardens
1–7 salina (salt works)
1 thorn house (graduation house)
2 thorns (brushwood)
3 brine channels
4 brine pipe from the pumping
station
5 salt works attendant
6–7 inhalational therapy
6 open–air inhalatorium (outdoor
inhalatorium)
7 patient inhaling (taking an
inhalation)
8 hydropathic (pump room) with
kursaal (casino)
9 colonnade
10 spa promenade
11 avenue leading to the mineral
spring
12–14 rest cure
12 sunbathing area (lawn)
13 deck–chair
14 sun canopy
15 pump room

16 rack for glasses
17 tap
18 patient taking the waters
19 bandstand
20 spa orchestra giving a concert
21 conductor

1–26 café, *sim.:* espresso bar, tea room
1 counter (cake counter)
2 coffee urn
3 tray for the money
4 gateau
5 meringue with whipped cream
6 trainee pastry cook
7 counter assistant
8 newspaper shelves (newspaper rack)
9 wall lamp
10 corner seat, an upholstered seat
11 café table
12 marble top
13 waitress
14 tray
15 bottle of lemonade
16 lemonade glass
17 chess players playing a game of chess
18 coffee set
19 cup of coffee
20 small sugar bowl
21 cream jug (*Am.* creamer)

22–24 café customers
22 gentleman
23 lady
24 man reading a newspaper
25 newspaper
26 newspaper holder

122 Restaurant

1–29 restaurant
1–11 bar (counter)
1 beer pump (beerpull)
2 drip tray
3 beer glass
4 froth (head)
5 spherical ashtray for cigarette and cigar ash
6 beer glass (beer mug)
7 beer warmer
8 bartender (barman, *Am.* barkeeper, barkeep)
9 shelf for glasses
10 shelf for bottles
11 stack of plates
12 coat stand
13 hat peg
14 coat hook
15 wall ventilator
16 bottle
17 complete meal
18 waitress
19 tray
20 lottery ticket seller
21 menu (menu card)

22 cruet stand
23 toothpick holder
24 matchbox holder
25 customer
26 beer mat
27 meal of the day
28 flower seller (flower girl)
29 flower basket
30–44 wine restaurant (wine bar)
30 wine waiter, a head waiter
31 wine list
32 wine carafe
33 wineglass
34 tiled stove
35 stove tile
36 stove bench
37 wooden panelling (*Am.* paneling)
38 corner seat
39 corner table
40 regular customer
41 cutlery chest
42 wine cooler
43 bottle of wine
44 ice cubes (ice, lumps of ice)

45–78 self–service restaurant
45 stack of trays
46 drinking straws (straws)
47 serviettes (napkins)
48 cutlery holders
49 cool shelf
50 slice of honeydew melon
51 plate of salad
52 plate of cheeses
53 fish dish
54 filled roll
55 meat dish with trimmings
56 half chicken
57 basket of fruit
58 fruit juice
59 drinks shelf
60 bottle of milk
61 bottle of mineral water
62 vegetarian meal (diet meal)
63 tray
64 tray counter
65 food price list
66 serving hatch
67 hot meal
68 beer pump (beerpull)

69 cash desk
70 cashier
71 proprietor
72 rail
73 dining area
74 table
75 open sandwich
76 ice–cream sundae
77 salt cellar and pepper pot
78 table decoration (flower arrangement)

123 Hotel

1-26 **vestibule** (foyer, reception hall)
1 doorman (commissionaire)
2 letter rack with pigeon holes
3 key rack
4 globe lamp, a frosted glass globe
5 indicator board (drop board)
6 indicator light
7 chief receptionist
8 register (hotel register)
9 room key
10 number tag (number tab) showing room number
11 hotel bill
12 block of registration forms
13 passport
14 hotel guest
15 lightweight suitcase, a light suitcase for air travel
16 wall desk
17 porter (*Am.* baggage man)
18-26 lobby (hotel lobby)
18 page (pageboy, *Am.* bell boy)
19 hotel manager
20 dining room (hotel restaurant)

21 chandelier
22 fireside
23 fireplace
24 mantelpiece (mantelshelf)
25 fire (open fire)
26 armchair
27-38 **hotel room**, a double room with bath
27 double door
28 service bell panel
29 wardrobe trunk
30 clothes compartment
31 linen compartment
32 double washbasin
33 room waiter
34 room telephone
35 velour (velours) carpet
36 flower stand
37 flower arrangement
38 double bed
39 **banquet room**
40-43 private party
40 speaker proposing a toast
41 42's neighbour (*Am.* neighbor)
42 43's partner

43 42's partner
44–46 **thé dansant** (tea dance) in the foyer
44 bar trio
45 violinist
46 couple dancing (dancing couple)
47 waiter
48 napkin
49 cigar and cigarette boy
50 cigarette tray
51 **hotel bar**
52 foot rail
53 bar stool
54 bar
55 bar customer
56 cocktail glass (*Am.* highball glass)
57 whisky (whiskey) glass
58 champagne cork
59 champagne bucket (champagne cooler)
60 measuring beaker (measure)
61 cocktail shaker
62 bartender (barman, *Am.* barkeeper, barkeep)
63 barmaid
64 shelf for bottles
65 shelf for glasses
66 mirrored panel
67 ice bucket

124 Town (Town Centre, *Am.* Downtown)

1 parking meter
2 map of the town (street map)
3 illuminated board
4 key
5 litter bin (*Am.* litter basket)
6 street lamp (street light)
7 street sign showing the name of the street
8 drain
9 clothes shop (fashion house)
10 shop window
11 window display (shop window display)
12 window decoration (shop window decoration)
13 entrance
14 window
15 window box
16 neon sign
17 tailor's workroom
18 pedestrian
19 shopping bag
20 road sweeper (*Am.* street sweeper)
21 broom

22 rubbish (litter)
23 tramlines (*Am.* streetcar tracks)
24 pedestrian crossing (zebra crossing, *Am.* crosswalk)
25 tram stop (*Am.* streetcar stop, trolley stop)
26 tram stop sign (*Am.* streetcar stop sign, trolley stop sign)
27 tram timetable (*Am.* streetcar schedule)
28 ticket machine
29 'pedestrian crossing' sign
30 traffic policeman on traffic duty (point duty)
31 traffic control cuff
32 white cap
33 hand signal
34 motorcyclist
35 motorcycle
36 pillion passenger (pillion rider)
37 bookshop
38 hat shop (hatter's shop); *for ladies' hats:* milliner's shop
39 shop sign
40 insurance company office

41 department store
42 shop front
43 advertisement
44 flags
45 illuminated letters
46 tram (*Am.* streetcar, trolley)
47 furniture lorry (*Am.* furniture truck)
48 flyover
49 suspended street lamp
50 stop line
51 pedestrian crossing (*Am.* crosswalk)
52 traffic lights
53 traffic light post
54 set of lights
55 pedestrian lights
56 telephone box (telephone booth, telephone kiosk, call box)
57 cinema advertisement (film poster)
58 pedestrian precinct (paved zone)
59 street café
60 group seated (sitting) at a table
61 sunshade

62 steps to the public lavatories (public conveniences)
63 taxi rank (taxi stand)
64 taxi (taxicab, cab)
65 taxi sign
66 traffic sign showing 'taxi rank' ('taxi stand')
67 taxi telephone
68 post office
69 cigarette machine
70 advertising pillar
71 poster (advertisement)
72 white line
73 lane arrow for turning left
74 lane arrow for going straight ahead
75 news vendor (*Am.* news dealer)

Ordering of Entries

In the index the entries are ordered as follows:
1. Entries consisting of single words, e.g.: 'hair'.
2. Entries consisting of noun + adjective. Within this category the adjectives are entered alphabetically, e.g. 'hair, bobbed' is followed by 'hair, closely-cropped'.

   Where adjective and noun are regarded as elements of a single lexical item, they are not inverted, e.g.: 'blue spruce', not 'spruce, blue'.
3. Entries consisting of other phrases, e.g. 'hair curler', 'ham on the bone', are alphabetized as headwords.

Where a whole phrase makes the meaning or use of a headword highly specific, the whole phrase is entered alphabetically. For example 'ham on the bone' follows 'hammock'.

Index

References
The numbers in bold type refer to the sections in which the word may be found, and those in normal type refer to the items named in the pictures. Homonyms, and in some cases uses of the same word in different fields, are distinguished by section headings (in italics), some of which are abbreviated, to help to identify at a glance the field required. In most cases the full form referred to by the abbreviations will be obvious. Those which are not are explained in the following list:

Agr.	Agriculture/Agricultural	*Hydr. Eng.*	Hydraulic Engineering
Alp. Plants	Alpine Plants	*Impl.*	Implements
Art. Studio	Artist's Studio	*Inf. Tech.*	Information Technology
Bldg.	Building	*Intern. Combust. Eng.*	Internal Combustion Engine
Carp.	Carpenter	*Moon L.*	Moon Landing
Cement Wks.	Cement Works	*Music Not.*	Musical Notation
Cost.	Costumes	*Overh. Irrign.*	Overhead Irrigation
Cyc.	Cycle	*Platem.*	Platemaking
Decid.	Deciduous	*Plant. Propagn.*	Propagation of Plants
D.I.Y.	Do-it-yourself	*Rm.*	Room
Dom. Anim.	Domestic Animals	*Sp.*	Sports
Equest.	Equestrian Sport	*Text.*	Textile[s]
Gdn.	Garden	*Veg.*	Vegetable[s]

athletics **95**
Atlas **15** 36
atomic pile casing **66** 67
atrium *Art* **15** 66
attack **2** 27
attack area **90** 64
attacker *Ball Games* **89** 3
attacker *Fencing* **91** 5
attacking fencer **91** 5
attack line **90** 65
attack periscope **66** 88
attic **38** 1-29, 18; **15** 60
attitude **111** 17
aubretia **51** 7
audience **70** 8
auditorium **112** 14-27, 16-20
auditorium lighting control **109**
    17
augmented triad **2** 4
aulos **3** 3
aulos pipe **3** 4
aureus **59** 3
Australopithecus **68** 20
auxiliaries **65** 92-97
auxiliary engine room **66** 56
avalanche **101** 1
avalanche forest **101** 7
avalanche gallery **101** 3
avalanche wall **101** 2
avalanche wedge **101** 2
Ave Maria **13** 32
avenue **120** 11
avionics bay, front ~ **64** 11
avionics bay, rear ~ **64** 18
awning *Camping* **75** 28, 37
awning *Dwellings* **37** 71
axe, bronze ~ **9** 23
axe, socketed ~ **9** 23
azalea **53** 12
azimuth **56** 74
azure *Heraldry* **61** 28

B

baby **28** 5
baby bath **28** 3
baby carriage **28** 34; **118** 71; **119**
    31
baby clothes **29** 1-12
baby doll **48** 25
baby grand piano **6** 40
baby pants **28** 22
baby pants, rubber ~ **29** 10
baby powder **28** 14
back *Ball Games* **90** 77
back *Sports* **102** 11
back *Swim.* **79** 49
back *Tablew. etc.* **45** 56
backboard **89** 30
back check **6** 27
back check felt **6** 28
backcloth **112** 33; **113** 10
back crease **89** 71
back cushion **42** 25
backdrop **112** 33; **113** 10
backdrop light **113** 15
back flip **94** 24
backgammon **73** 18
backgammon board **73** 22

background *Films* **107** 33
background *Theatre* **113** 10
backhand stroke **90** 39
back left second pin **102** 9
back loop **85** 50
back pin **102** 11
back right second pin **102** 10
back sight leaf **56** 67
back sight slide **56** 69
back support **92** 22; **93** 29
back-up ball **102** 20
back vault **94** 32
backward grand circle **93** 60
backward somersault *Gymn.* **94**
    15
backward somersault *Swim.* **79** 42
backward underswing **93** 59
backward walkover **94** 23
badge, fool's ~ **103** 60
badger **57** 48
badminton **90** 43-44
badminton game **119** 6
badminton racket **90** 43
badminton racquet **90** 43
baffle board **106** 17
baffle board, hinged ~ **66** 15
baffle board, movable ~ **66** 15
baffle board *Warships* **66** 27
bag-full indicator **50** 61, 73
baggage compartment **64** 19
baggage man **123** 17
bag *Hunt.* **55** 38
bag *Music. Instr.* **3** 9
bag, girl's ~ **29** 56
bagpipe **3** 8
bag sealer **40** 47
bag wig **34** 4
bail **89** 70
bailey, inner ~ **10** 2
bailey, outer ~ **10** 31
bait **55** 21
bait needle **58** 41
baits **58** 65-76
bait, weighted ~ **58** 36
bait tin **58** 24
balalaika **5** 28
balancer **104** 48
balance rail **3** 39
balancing act **104** 44
balancing pole **104** 42
balcony *Chivalry* **10** 12
balcony *Dwellings* **37** 18, 69, 73
balcony *Theatre* **112** 16; **112** 18
baldachin **12** 49
baldaquin **12** 49
bald patch **34** 21
bale arm **58** 62
ballast *Airsports* **85** 65
ballast keel **82** 32
ballast *Sailing* **82** 33
ball *Ball Games* **89** 27
ball *Circus* **104** 50
ball *Infant Care etc.* **28** 16
ball, ivory ~ **74** 1
ball, metal ~ **24** 32
ball, paper ~ **103** 55
ball, plastic ~ **74** 1
ball, stone ~ **24** 32
ball boy **90** 22
ballerina **111** 26

ballet **111**
ballet dancer **111** 26
ballet positions **111** 1-6
ballet shoe **111** 30
ballet skirt **111** 31
ballet slipper **111** 30
ball games **88**; **89**; **90**
ballistics **56** 73
balloon **105** 13
balloon basket **85** 64
balloon, gas ~ **85** 63
balloon, hot-air ~ **85** 79
ballooning **85** 63-84
ballot box **70** 29
ballot envelope **70** 21
ballot paper **70** 20
ballroom **103** 1
baluster **38** 29
balustrade **38** 25
bandage *Equest.* **86** 15
band *Ball Games* **88** 25
band *Church* **13** 5
band *Nightclub* **115** 3
banderilla **116** 22
banderillero **116** 4, 21
band, ornamental ~ **15** 38
bandoneon **5** 36
bandora **3** 21
bandstand **120** 19; **104** 9
banger **103** 51
bangle *Ethnol.* **26** 38
bangle *Jewell.* **36** 17
bangle, asymmetrical ~ **36** 26
bangs **34** 36
banjo **5** 29
bank *Roulette* **72** 11
banknotes **59** 29-39
bank of circulation **59** 30
bank of issue **59** 30
banner *Election* **70** 12
banner *Flags* **60** 12
banner, processional ~ **12** 44
banquet room **123** 39
baptism, Christian ~ **13** 1
baptistery **13** 2
bar *Athletics* **95** 14, 34
bar *Circus* **104** 50
bar *Disco* **114** 1, 9
bar *Graphic Art* **21** 34
bar *Gymn.* **93** 3, 8; **94** 4, 41
bar *Hotel* **123** 54
bar *Music. Not.* **1** 42
bar *Nightclub* **115** 13, 15
bar *Park* **118** 34
bar *Playground* **119** 32
bar *Restaurant* **122** 1-11
bar *Winter Sp.* **100** 5
bar, metal ~ **5** 77
bar arm **96** 10
barbecue **75** 47
barb *Fish Farm.* **58** 80
bar customer **123** 55
bareback rider **104** 26
bargeboard **37** 8
barkeep **122** 8; **123** 62
barkeeper **122** 8; **123** 62
barker **105** 8, 64
bar lamp **114** 11
bar line **1** 42
barmaid **123** 63; **111** 2; **115** 14

bell tent **75** 8
bell tower **18** 8
belly *Music. Instr.* **4** 24; **5** 3
belt **30** 11; **31** 10; **32** 39
belt buckle **31** 12
belt-changing flap **62** 35
belt, coloured ~ **96** 15
belt, stretch ~ **31** 63
bench *Playground* **119** 58
bench, oarsman's ~ **75** 17
bench, pupil's ~ **68** 11
bench, student's ~ **68** 11
bench, teacher's ~ **68** 3
bench, tiered ~ **78** 20
bend of hook **58** 81
bend sinister wavy **61** 6
bent hang **93** 39
beret **35** 27
Bermuda shorts **31** 44
berry bush **52** 19
berry tree, standard ~ **52** 11
besageur **10** 45
besom *Roof & Boilerr.* **38** 36
besom *Winter Sp.* **99** 43
bez antler **57** 7
bez tine **57** 7
B flat major **1** 64
B flat minor **1** 67
bib *Infant Care etc.* **28** 43
bib *Ladies' Wear* **30** 24
bib and brace *Child. Clothes* **29** 40
bib and brace *Ladies' Wear* **30** 21
bib and brace overalls **33** 44
Bible **11** 11
bib skirt **29** 41
bicycle, childgrs ~ **119** 9
bicycle kick **88** 45
bidet **49** 7
Biedermeier dress **103** 22
Biedermeier sofa **17** 17
bier **12** 41
big top **104** 1
big wave riding **76** 4
big wheel **105** 37
bikini **77** 26
bikini bottom **77** 27
bikini briefs **32** 15
bikini top **77** 28
bill *Game* **57** 84
billiard ball **74** 1
billiard clock **74** 17
billiard cloth **74** 15
billiard cue **74** 9
billiard marker **74** 18
billiard parlor **74** 7-19
billiard player **74** 8
billiard room **74** 7-19
billiards **74** 1-19
billiard saloon **74** 7-19
billiards, English ~ **74** 7
billiards, French ~ **74** 7
billiards, German ~ **74** 7
billiard stick **74** 9
billiard strokes **74** 2-6
billiard table **74** 14
bills **59** 29-39
bind **2** 24
binding *Athletics* **95** 54
binding, parts of ~ **98** 54-56

binding, rubber ~ **83** 57-58
binoculars **55** 6
biology preparation room **68** 14-34
bipod **62** 42
birch **51** 13; **118** 40; **78** 27
birch rod **78** 27
birch tree **51** 13; **118** 40
bird **55** 50
biscuit tin, decorative ~ **46** 12
bishop **73** 10
bison **9** 9
bitt **81** 25
blackboard, three-part ~ **67** 29
blackboard **47** 13; **48** 16; **68** 36
blackboard chalk **48** 15
blackboard compass **67** 40
blackboard drawing **67** 33
blackboard sponge **67** 42
blackcock **55** 11; **57** 66
blade *Fencing* **91** 44
blade *Kitch. Utensils* **40** 40
blade *Rowing* **80** 38, 53
blade *Tablew. etc.* **45** 54
blade covering **90** 47
blade, rotating ~ **39** 24
blank **59** 43
blazer **33** 54
blazing star **51** 31
blazon **61** 17-23
blazonry **61** 1-36
bleeder **38** 65
blender **40** 46
Blessed Sacrament **12** 48; **13** 35
blimp **107** 48; **110** 16-18, 27
blind *Hunt.* **55** 9
block *Headgear* **35** 3
block *Music. Instr.* **7** 20
block, adjustable ~ **95** 2
block, wooden ~ **21** 1
blocker **90** 60
block of flats **37** 72-76
block of flats, high-rise ~ **37** 82
block of flats, multi-storey ~ **37** 77-81
blotter **46** 23; **67** 25
blouse **30** 9
blouse, girl's ~ **29** 58
blowlamp **98** 22
blowout magnet **109** 39
blowpipe *Ethnol.* **24** 26
blow, straight ~ **96** 28
blowtorch **98** 22
blubber-oil lamp **25** 7
blue light **71** 11
Blue Peter **60** 26
blue spruce **51** 10
B minor **1** 57, 60
board *Games* **73** 1
board games **73**
board, illuminated ~ **124** 3
board, presawn ~ **119** 57
board, wooden ~ **19** 23
boarding, horizontal ~ **37** 84
boar *Game* **57** 51
boar, young ~ **57** 51
boarhound **55** 33
boar hunt **55** 31
boat, carvel-built ~ **80** 9

boat, inflatable ~ **65** 82; **75** 14; **76** 27
boat, ship's ~ **65** 12, 45; **66** 35
boat, V-bottom ~ **83** 35-37
boat, vee-bottom ~ **83** 35-37
boat axe **9** 19
boat carriage **75** 20; **80** 66
boater **35** 35
boat fibula **9** 28
boathouse **80** 24
boat-launching crane **65** 13
boat neck **30** 34
boats, folding ~ **80** 54-66
boat trailer **75** 20; **80** 66
bobble **29** 4
boblet **100** 19
bobsled **100** 19
bobsledding **100** 19-21
bobsleigh **100** 19-21
bobsleigh, two-man ~ **100** 19
bob wig **34** 2
boccie **102** 21
bodhisattva **18** 10
bodice **31** 30
bodkin beard **34** 13
body *Airsports* **85** 26
body, bird's ~ **8** 57
body, dog's ~ **8** 30
body, dragon's ~ **8** 19, 36
body, horse's ~ **8** 27, 54
body, lion's ~ **8** 14, 22
body, man's ~ **8** 53
body, monster's ~ **8** 48
body, serpent's ~ **8** 2, 33
body. tambourine-like ~ **5** 30
body, woman's ~ **8** 59
body plan **66** 2-11
body rotation **95** 11
boiler *Roof & Boilerr.* **38** 24, 68
boiler room *Roof & Boilerr.* **38** 38-43
boiler suit **30** 21
bola **24** 31
bolas **24** 31
bolster *Bedrm.* **43** 11
bolster *Tablew. etc.* **45** 55
bolt handle **56** 22
bolt lever **56** 22
bombard **3** 14
bombardon **4** 44
bomber jacket **31** 42
bone **26** 40
bongo drum **5** 58
book **42** 4; **46** 8
book, children's ~ **47** 17; **48** 23
book, second-hand ~ **106** 55
bookcase unit **46** 7
bookshelf **42** 3; **43** 14; **69** 12
bookshelf unit **46** 7
bookshop **124** 37
book stack **69** 11
boomerang **24** 39
boom *Sailing* **81** 7, 39
boom microphone **108** 40
boom operator **107** 22
boomswinger **107** 22
bootee **28** 45; **29** 5
boot *Music. Instr.* **7** 17
boot, felt ~ **25** 30
booth **105** 6

bootlace **88** 32
boot, rubber ~ **86** 32
border *Fruit & Veg. Gdn.* **52** 18, 22
border light **113** 13
border *Park* **118** 37
border *Theatre* **113** 12
bore axis **56** 38
bore diameter **56** 40
borrower's ticket **69** 25
boscage **118** 4
boss *Art* **16** 32
boss *Chivalry* **10** 58
bottle *Restaurant* **122** 16
bottle *Swim.* **76** 19
bottle-opener **45** 47
bottle rack *Kitch.* **39** 6
bottlescrew **81** 19
bottle warmer **28** 21
bottom, artificial ~ **98** 52
bottom, synthetic ~ **98** 52
bottom fishing **58** 20-31
boudoir piano **6** 40
boule, grooved ~ **102** 24
boules **102** 21
boules player **102** 22
bounce **94** 36
bouncing ball **119** 20
boundary layer control flap **63** 6; **64** 13
bouquet, bridal ~ **13** 18
bout **91** 5-6
bow *Ethnol.* **26** 32
bow *Hairst. etc.* **34** 7
bow *Hist. Cost.* **27** 78
bow *Ladies' Wear* **30** 46
bow *Music. Instr.* **4** 12
bow *Rowing* **80** 13
bow, fully enclosed ~ **66** 9
bow and arrow **8** 53
bow bilge **66** 80
bowed instruments **4** 1-27
bower **118** 17
bower anchor **65** 39; **83** 15
bower, ladies' ~ **10** 10
bow gin **56** 48
bowl **40** 6; **45** 63
bowler **89** 76
bow light, green and red ~ **83** 13
bowling ball **102** 15
bowling crease **89** 71
bowls **102** 21
bow ramp **65** 90
bow stick **4** 14
bow string **102** 59
bow-tie **32** 47; **33** 11, 16
bow trap **56** 48
box *Athletics* **95** 35
box *Bullfight. etc.* **116** 7
box *Fair* **105** 7
box *Gymn.* **93** 15
box, coach's ~ **89** 56
box, racer's ~ **87** 7
box, rider's ~ **87** 7
box, small ~ **93** 16; **94** 9
box attendant **112** 12
box camera **106** 30
boxer *Sports* **96** 25
boxing **96** 20-50

boxing contest **96** 35-50
boxing glove **96** 26
boxing match **96** 20-50
boxing ring **96** 35
box office **105** 7
box room door **38** 20
box spar **84** 30
box trap **55** 20
boy scout **75** 11
bra **32** 1; **115** 29
bra, longline ~ **32** 4
bracelet **36** 3
bracelet, cultured pearl ~ **36** 9
bracelet, gemstone ~ **36** 25
bracelet watch **36** 33
brace *Music. Instr.* **6** 16
braces **29** 26, 34; **32** 30
braces, adjustable ~ **33** 45
braces clip **32** 31
bracket *School* **67** 30
bracket *Winter Sp.* **99** 17; **100** 7
bracket, round ~ **23** 24
bracket, square ~ **23** 25
bracteate **59** 4
braid, floral ~ **30** 28
Braille **23** 15
brake *Air Force* **64** 10
brake chute housing **64** 24
brake flap *Air Force* **63** 12
brake flap *Gliding* **84** 38
brakeman **100** 21
brandy glass **45** 88
brass **4** 39-48
brassard *Chivalry* **10** 47
brassie **90** 91
brassière **32** 1; **115** 29
brassière, longline ~ **32** 4
brass instruments **4** 39-48
bratwurst **105** 34
brayer **21** 12
bread **45** 22
bread and cheese **122** 75
bread basket **45** 20
breaker *Swim.* **76** 6
breakwater *Warships* **65** 7, 76
breastplate **10** 46
breast pocket **33** 9
breaststroke **79** 33
breastwork **10** 24
breeches **97** 7
breeches, loose ~ **27** 34
breeches, white ~ **86** 5
breech ring **62** 54
breve **1** 12
breve rest **1** 20
breviary **12** 58
brevis **1** 12
bride **13** 15
bridegroom **13** 16
bridesmaid **13** 24
bridge *Free Exerc.* **92** 19
bridge *Music. Instr.* **3** 17
bridge *Park* **118** 47
bridge *Sports* **96** 9
bridge *Theatre* **112** 29; **113** 34
bridge *Warships* **65** 14; **66** 3, 28
bridge ring **58** 58
bridge superstructure **65** 14
briefcase **41** 17
briefs **32** 26

brille **4** 35
brilliant cut **36** 44
brine channel **120** 3
brine pipe **120** 4
briolette, faceted ~ **36** 86
bristle **57** 52
bristles *Hairst. etc.* **34** 23
bristles *Household* **50** 47
broadsheet **21** 27
broadside **21** 27
broadtail *Ladies' Wear* **30** 60
broiler **105** 33
Bronze Age **9** 21-40
brooch, ivory ~ **36** 30
brooch, modern-style ~ **36** 19
brooch, pearl ~ **36** 7
brood bud bulblet **54** 27, 29
broom **38** 36; **50** 46; **124** 21; **118** 67
broom handle **38** 37; **50** 49
broom head **50** 48
broomstick **38** 37; **50** 49
brow antler **57** 6
brow point **57** 6
brow snag **57** 6
brow tine **57** 6
brush *Game* **57** 47
brush *Graphic Art* **21** 11
brush *Household* **50** 42, 53
brush *Roof & Boilerr.* **38** 32
brush *School* **67** 59
brush *Script* **22** 24
brush, camel hair ~ **19** 7
brush, flat ~ *Art Studio* **19** 6
brush, round ~ **19** 8
brush head **50** 79
brush head, detachable ~ **49** 30
brush, wire ~ *Music. Instr.* **5** 53
brushwood *Spa* **120** 2
bubble bath **49** 3
bubble float, oval ~ **58** 47
buccaneer **103** 43
bucket *Household* **50** 54
bucket seat *Sports* **102** 90
bucket-top boot **27** 58
buck *Game* **57** 28, 40, 59
buck *Gymn.* **93** 17
buckler **10** 57
buck, young ~ **57** 39
bud **54** 23, 26
bud cutting **54** 22
Buddha **18** 20
budding **54** 30
budding knife **54** 31
buffalo horn **61** 34
buffer *Army* **62** 27, 44, 52
buffer recuperator **62** 52
buffer ring **62** 44
buffoon **103** 38, 69
bugle **106** 54
building block **28** 41; **48** 27
building brick *Infant Care etc.* **28** 41
building brick *Kindergart.* **48** 27
building, centralized ~ **15** 55
building, centrally-planned ~ **15** 55
building, model ~ **48** 28
building, neoclassical ~ **17** 15
built piece **112** 32

chemistry laboratory **68** 1
chemistry teacher **68** 2
chequer-board cut **36** 66
cherub **118** 20
chess **121** 17; **73** 1-16
chessboard **47** 20; **73** 1
chessboard square **73** 2
chess championship **73** 16
chess clock **73** 16
chessman **73** 1, 4, 5, 7
chess match **73** 16
chess move **73** 6
chess player **121** 17
chess problem **73** 6
chess square **73** 6
chest of drawers **41** 8
chevron design **16** 16
chief **61** 18-19
chignon **34** 29
child **67** 3
child, small ~ **28** 42
children's room **47**
chimera **8** 16
chimney *Dwellings.* **37** 10
chimney *Mountain.* **97** 8
chimney *Roof & Boilerr.* **38** 5
chimney sweep **38** 31
chimney sweeper **38** 31
china, broken ~ **67** 61
china cabinet **44** 26
chinband **27** 22
Chinese lantern **52** 15
chine strake **65** 8
chin rest **4** 8
chintuft **34** 10
chip *Roulette* **72** 12
chip pan **40** 41
chisel, bevelled-edge ~ **20** 19
chisel, flat ~ **20** 14
chisel, hollow ~ **20** 17
chisel, toothed ~ **20** 13
chitarrone **5** 1
chiton **27** 5
chivalry **10**
choir **11** 32; **16** 4
choir organ **7** 5, 42
choke cymbals **5** 50
choker **36** 16
choker collar **27** 74
chord *Music. Not.* **2** 1-5, 5
chorus **112** 21
christening **13** 1
christening dress **13** 8
christening robe **13** 8
christening shawl **13** 9
Christian **11** 61
chromatic scale **1** 49
chromolithograph **21** 28
chrysanthemum **51** 29
church **11**; **12** 1; **13**
church, Baroque ~ **17** 1
church, Gothic ~ **16** 22
church, Protestant ~ **11** 1-30
church, Renaissance ~ **16** 42
church, Roman Catholic ~ **11** 31-62
church, Romanesque ~ **16** 1-13
church banner **12** 44
church clock **12** 7
church door *Art* **16** 24

church door *Church* **12** 16
churchgoer **11** 29; **12** 17
church organ **7** 1-52
church roof **12** 11
church spire **12** 6
church wedding **13** 14
church window **11** 14
churchyard **12** 21-41
churchyard gate **12** 19
churchyard wall **12** 18
chute *Fair* **105** 40
ciborium **13** 48
cigar and cigarette boy **123** 49
cigarette machine **124** 69
cigarette seller **105** 51
cigarette tray **123** 50
cinema **109** 1
cinema, mobile ~ **109** 52
cinema advertisement **124** 57
cinema audience **109** 5
cinema box office **109** 2
cinemagoer **109** 5
cinema projector **109** 24
cinema projector, narrow-gauge
~ **109** 52
cinemascope camera **107** 47
cinema ticket **109** 3
cine projector **115** 20
cinquefoil **16** 40
circle *Sports* **102** 31
circle, inner ~ **85** 57
circle, middle ~ **85** 58
circle, outer ~ **85** 59
circle, upper ~ **112** 17
circling engagement **91** 49
circuit breaker, miniature ~ **41**
20
circumflex **23** 32
circus **104**
circus, travelling ~ **104** 1-63
circus act **104** 25
circus attendant **104** 27
circus band **104** 10
circus box **104** 16
circus caravan **104** 34
circus horse **104** 30
circus manager **104** 17
circus marksman **104** 38
circus rider **104** 26
circus tent **104** 1
circus trailer **104** 34
cistern **49** 16
cist, long ~ **9** 16
cist, stone ~ **9** 17
cithara **3** 15
cittern **3** 21
city wall **14** 30
clapper *Carnival* **103** 47
clapper *Films* **107** 35
clapper board **107** 35
clapper boy **107** 34
claque **35** 36
clarinet **115** 4; **4** 34
clarinettist **115** 5
clasp, white gold ~ **36** 10
classroom **67** 1-45
classroom cupboard **67** 43
clavicembalo **3** 45
clavichord **3** 36
clavichord mechanism **3** 37

clavilux **114** 13
claw **8** 3
claw, bird's ~ **8** 61
claw chisel **20** 13
claws, griffin's ~ **8** 13
clay **67** 79; **20** 8, 31
clay box **20** 30
clay pigeon shooting **102** 70-78
cleaning brush *Hunt.* **56** 62
cleaning rag **50** 55
cleaning rod **56** 61
cleaning tow **56** 63
cleanout door **38** 39
cleansing pond **58** 6
clearstory **15** 70
clefs **1** 8-11
clench planking **82** 50-52
clerestory **15** 70
clergyman **11** 22; **12** 37; **13** 22
clergyman, Protestant ~ **13** 3
clerk **70** 26, 27
clew **81** 41
climber *Flower Gdn.* **51** 5
climber *Fruit & Veg. Gdn.* **52** 5
climber *Indoor Plants* **53** 2
climber *Mountain.* **97** 5
climbing **97** 2-13
climbing boot **97** 44
climbing breeches **97** 7
climbing equipment **97** 31-57
climbing frame **119** 47
climbing harness **97** 56
climbing net **119** 50
climbing plant **53** 2
climbing roof **119** 60
climbing rope **119** 48; **93** 19
climbing tower **119** 17
clinch **96** 31
clinker planking **82** 50-52
Clivia minata **53** 8
cloak **27** 18, 26
cloak, red ~ **116** 27
cloak, short ~ **27** 29
cloak, Spanish ~ **27** 29
cloak cord **27** 24
cloakroom **48** 34; **112** 5; **115** 1
cloakroom attendant **112** 6; **115** 2
cloakroom hall **112** 5-11
cloakroom ticket **112** 7
cloak woollen ~ **27** 6
cloche **35** 12
clock, double ~ **73** 16
clock case **106** 57
clog **27** 43
cloister **12** 52
cloister vault **17** 41
closed vertical gate **98** 66
cloth, damask ~ **45** 2
clothes, children's ~ **29**
clothes, teenagers' ~ **29** 48-68
clothes brush **50** 44
clothes closet **43** 1
clothes closet door **46** 2
clothes compartment **123** 30
clothes line **38** 23; **50** 33
clothes rack **117** 31
clothes shop **124** 9
cloth **117** 59
cloth, felt ~ **21** 42
cloud, lenticular ~ **84** 19

clown **103** 69; **104** 24
clown, musical ~ **104** 23
clown act **104** 25
club **80** 23
clubhouse **80** 23
club membership **83** 8
clubs **73** 38
C major **1** 55, 62
C major scale **1** 45
C minor **1** 65
coach *Ball Games* **88** 55; **89** 57
coal scuttle **106** 9
coal shovel **38** 43
coaming **80** 59
coarse dirt hose **50** 84
coarse fishing **58** 20-31
coastal cruiser **81** 60
coat **29** 54; **30** 60; **33** 2
coat, black ~ **86** 4
coat, cloth ~ **30** 61; **33** 66
coat, dark ~ **86** 4, 13
coat, fur ~ **30** 60
coat, loden ~ **30** 64
coat, loose-fitting ~ **117** 41
coat, poncho-style ~ **30** 68
coat, poplin ~ **33** 60
coat, red ~ **86** 13
coat, three-quarter length ~ **117** 21
coat belt **33** 59
coat button **33** 64
coat collar **33** 58
coat hanger **41** 3
coat hook **41** 2; **122** 14
coat-of-arms **61** 1-6
coat-of-arms, marshalled ~ **61** 10-13
coat-of-arms, provincial ~ **59** 12, 14
coat pocket **33** 61
coat rack **41** 1
coat stand **122** 12
coat-tail **33** 14
cockade **71** 8
cockatrice **8** 34
cocking handle **62** 12
cocking lever **62** 12
cock pheasant **57** 77
cockpit *Airsports* **85** 10
cockpit *Police* **71** 2
cockpit *Rowing* **80** 8
cockpit *Sailing* **82** 38
cockpit canopy **64** 4
cockpit coaming **80** 59
cockpit hood **64** 4
cocktail **114** 33
cocktail fork **45** 76
cocktail glass **123** 56
cocktail shaker **123** 61
cocotte **103** 37
code pendant **60** 29
code pennant **60** 29
coffee **121** 19
coffee cup **44** 29
coffee grinder, electric ~ **39** 24
coffee maker **39** 38
coffee pot **44** 28
coffee service **44** 27
coffee set **44** 27; **121** 18
coffee table **42** 28

coffee urn **121** 2
cofferdam **66** 19
coffin **12** 35
coffin chamber **14** 5
coiffures **34** 27-38
coiffure, upswept ~ **27** 81
coil **58** 21
coin **59** 1-28
coin, Celtic ~ **9** 37
coin, gold ~ **36** 37
coin, silver ~ **9** 37
coinage **59** 1-28, 40-44
coin bracelet **36** 36
coin disc **59** 43
coining dies **59** 40-41
coining press **59** 44
coins **59** 1-28
coins, aluminium ~ **59** 1-28
coins, copper ~ **59** 1-28
coin setting **36** 38
coins, gold ~ **59** 1-28
coins, nickel ~ **59** 1-28
coins, silver ~ **59** 1-28
collar *Church* **13** 6
collar *Game* **57** 27
collar *Jewell.* **36** 16
collar *Money* **59** 42
collar, cowl ~ **30** 3
collar, fur ~ **30** 63
collar, fur-trimmed ~ **30** 63
collar, high ~ **27** 74
collar, knitted ~ **33** 31
collar, stand-up ~ **30** 43
collar, turndown ~ **30** 5; **31** 6
collar, wide-falling ~ **27** 56
college **69** 1-25
college lecturer **69** 3
colon **23** 17
colonnade **120** 9; **334** 67
colophony **4** 11
colour filter **113** 49
colour medium **113** 49
colour organ **114** 13
colour print **21** 28
columbine *Carnival* **103** 27
column *Script* **23** 45
column, Corinthian ~ **15** 10
column, Doric ~ **15** 8
column heading **23** 46
column, Ionic ~ **15** 9
column, ornamented ~ **14** 18
column rule **23** 47
column shaft **15** 26
combat sports **96**
combination, two-piece ~ **30** 45
comb *Infant Care etc.* **28** 8
comic turn **104** 25
comma **23** 18
commissionaire **123** 1; **117** 44; **112** 10
committee **70** 1-2
committee boat **82** 15
committee member **70** 2
committee table **70** 3
common myrtle **53** 11
common pheasant **57** 77
common time **1** 32
communicant **13** 27
communion cup **11** 10; **13** 29

communion table **11** 4
communion wafer **13** 50
companion hatch **65** 24
companion ladder **65** 24
companionway **65** 24
compartment *Store* **117** 6
compartment batten **113** 13
compass *Airsports* **85** 12
compass, divisions of ~ **2** 42-50
compendium of games **47** 18
competition bow **102** 54
competitor **79** 28
composition *Art. Studio* **19** 4
compost heap **52** 6
comprehensive school **68** 1-45
compressed-air bottle **76** 21
compressed-air cylinder **76** 21
compressed-air pressure gauge **76** 13
concave ridge **99** 22
concert grand **6** 40
concertina **5** 36
conch shell trumpet **8** 41
concrete mixer **47** 40
condenser *Warships* **66** 64
conductor *Spa* **120** 21
conductor *Theatre* **112** 26
conduit **15** 54
cone chest **7** 12-14
confetti **103** 62
conga drum **5** 55
congregation **11** 29
connector fitting **84** 31
console *Music. Instr.* **7** 36-52
console *School* **68** 37
console piano **6** 1
construction, close-seamed ~ **82** 54
construction, wooden ~ **67** 72
construction set **48** 22
construction vehicle **62** 75
continuity girl **107** 39
contouche **27** 66
contour knife **21** 10
contrabass **4** 23
contrabassoon **4** 28
contrabass tuba **4** 44
contracted burial **9** 17
contra octave **2** 43
control, sliding ~ **108** 18
control and monitoring panel **108** 8
control arm **110** 11
control button *School* **68** 45
control cable **117** 53
control column **64** 8; **85** 14
control console *Films* **108** 12
control console *Theatre* **113** 2
control desk *Films* **108** 12
control frame **84** 46
control lever *Films* **110** 11
control lever *Theatre* **113** 58
control line model **85** 89
control loudspeaker **108** 13
control panel *Films* **108** 4, 17, 29
control panel *Roof & Boilerr.* **38** 67
control rod *Warships* **66** 69
control room *Theatre* **113** 1
controls **117** 48

ejection seat **64** 6, 7
ejector seat **64** 6, 7
elbow *Winter Sp.* **98** 70
elbow boot **86** 31
elbow pad **100** 16
election **70** 16-30
election meeting **70** 1-15
election officer **70** 17
election regulations **70** 25
election speaker **70** 5
election supervisor **70** 28
elector **70** 24
electoral register **70** 18
electric action organ **7** 36-52
electrical point **68** 12
electrical socket **68** 12
elephant, toy ~ **47** 6
elevating gear **62** 67
elevating piston **62** 51
elevator *Air Force* **64** 22
elevator *Airsports* **85** 24
elevator *Store* **117** 45
elevator *Theatre* **113** 33, 34
elevator car **117** 46
elevator controls **117** 48
elevator operator **117** 47
ellipsis **23** 29
E major **1** 59
embrasure **10** 18
embroidery **29** 29; **30** 42; **27** 67
emergency crash barrier **66** 17
emergency exit **104** 33; **109** 7
emergency lighting **109** 6
E minor **1** 56
Empire table **17** 16
empress, Byzantine ~ **27** 15
em rule **23** 23
enamelling **67** 62
enamelling stove, electric ~ **67** 63
enamel powder **67** 65
enclosure wall **10** 15
encyclopaedia **42** 18; **69** 17
end, west ~ **16** 22
end-grain block **21** 1
end line **89** 36
end ring **58** 52
endurance competition **86** 16
engagement **91** 46
engine *Airsports* **85** 35
engine, two-stroke ~ **102** 92
engine pod **63** 25
English *Billiards* **74** 5
English hand **23** 10
engraver **21** 16
engraving **36** 41
ensign of head of state **60** 14
ensign staff **65** 25
entablature **15** 52
entrance **104** 19
entrance, bullfighters' ~ **116** 10
entrance hall **41** 1-29
entrance, main ~ **116** 6
entrance, side ~ **12** 15; **16** 13
entrance tunnel **25** 6
entrechat **111** 22
epaulière **10** 44
épée **91** 25-33, 36
épée, electric ~ **91** 26
épéeist **91** 25
épée point **91** 27

epistyle **15** 18
equalizer **108** 19
equestrian sport **86**
equilibrist **104** 48
erase head **108** 25
erasing head **108** 25
escalator **117** 22
escapologist **105** 28
escudo **59** 23
Eskimo **25** 1
Eskimo kayak **80** 68
espalier **37** 33; **52** 1, 2, 16, 17, 29
espalier, free-standing ~ **52** 16
espalier fruit tree **52** 1, 2, 16, 17, 29
espresso bar **121** 1-26
esquire **10** 68
estoque **116** 32
etching **21** 14-24
etching bath **21** 51
etching ground **21** 55
etching needle **21** 16
ethnology **24**; **25**; **26**
evening dress **33** 13
evening gown **30** 53
evening suit **33** 7
excavator, toy ~ **119** 65
exciter lamp **109** 48
exclamation mark **23** 21
exclamation point **23** 21
exercise book **47** 24; **67** 4, 18
exercises **93** 48-60
exergue **59** 10
exhaust bubbles **76** 26
exhaust escape flue **65** 79
exhaust outlet **66** 92
exhaust pipe *Warships* **65** 44
exit **104** 19
exit gate **116** 12
exotic **103** 30
expansion tank **38** 24
experimental apparatus **68** 11
expression marks **2** 27-41
extension tube *Household* **50** 70
extra **107** 29; **113** 39
extraction vent **49** 20
extrados **17** 26
eye *Art* **15** 75
eye *Fish Farm.* **58** 82
eye *Game* **57** 15, 33, 43, 60
eyecup **10** 34
eyepiece control ring **110** 7
eyepiece **108** 9

F

fabled beings **8**
fabric *Store* **117** 59
fabric department **117** 58
fabulous creatures **8**
façade, west ~ **16** 22
face, metal ~ **100** 11
face guard **89** 11, 25
face mask *Swim.* **76** 10
face pipes **7** 1-3
face urn **9** 38
face vault **94** 30
facing, decorative ~ **30** 47
facsimile signature **59** 34

fair **105**
fair, annual ~ **105** 1-69
fairground **105** 1
fairlead **81** 29
fairy-tale figure **103** 65
falcon **55** 46
falconer **55** 42
falconry **55** 42-46
fallow buck **57** 40
fallow deer **57** 40-41
falls, artificial ~ **118** 9
family grave **12** 27
family tomb **12** 27
fancy appliqué **35** 7
fancy dress **103** 6-48, 32
fancy-dress ball **103** 1-48
fan *Ethnol.* **25** 42
fan *Game* **57** 75
fan *Roof & Boilerr.* **38** 58
fanlight **37** 35
fan vault **17** 46
fashion doll **47** 9; **48** 32
fashion house **124** 9
fashion journal **117** 36
fashion magazine **117** 36
fastening *Plant Propagn.* **54** 13
fat lady **105** 21
fattening pond **58** 6
faucet *Kitch.* **39** 36
faucet, outside ~ **37** 41
faustball **90** 72-78, 74
favorite **86** 52
favourite **86** 52
fawn **57** 39
fawn, female ~ **57** 34
F-clef **1** 9
feather *Chivalry* **10** 78
feather *Headgear* **35** 6, 12
feather, falcate ~ **57** 68
feather, peacock's ~ **61** 36
feeding bottle **28** 19
feeding place **55** 28
feed mechanism *Graphic Art* **21** 33
feed spindle **109** 36
feed sprocket **109** 26
feet-first jump **79** 13
felt pen **48** 18
felt tip pen **67** 19
fence *Equest.* **86** 8
fence *Swim.* **78** 17
fence, paling ~ **52** 10
fence, stone ~ **18** 23
fence, wooden ~ **37** 53
fencers **91** 5-6
fencer's salute **91** 18
fencing **91**
fencing glove **91** 12
fencing instructor **91** 1
fencing jacket **91** 16
fencing mask **91** 13, 14
fencing master **91** 1
fencing measure **91** 10
fencing, modern ~ **91** 1-33
fencing movement **91** 7
fencing shoe, heelless ~ **91** 17
fencing weapons **91** 34-45
ferret **55** 24
ferreter **55** 25
ferreting **55** 23

golfer **90** 83
golf trolley **90** 85
gondola *Airsports* **85** 64
gonfalon **60** 12
gong **96** 46
goods **117** 10
goods shelf **47** 36
gooseberry bush **52** 19
goose **118** 52
gooseneck **81** 37
gorgerin **15** 22
gorget **10** 43
gouache **19** 17
gouge **20** 17
gouge, U-shaped ~ **21** 6
gouge, V-shaped ~ **20** 20; **21** 9
gourd **26** 27
gown **27** 25, 36, 66
gown, linen ~ **27** 5
gown, open ~ **27** 50
gown, sleeveless ~ **27** 50
grace notes **2** 14-22
graces **2** 14-22
graduation house *Spa* **120** 1
graftage **54** 30-39
grafting **54** 30-39
grain *Graphic Art* **21** 47
grammar school **68** 1-45
gramophone **106** 31
gramophone box **106** 35
gramophone needle **106** 33
gramophone record **106** 32
grand **6** 40
grandee **103** 26
grandfather clock **106** 56
grand piano **6** 40
grand piano pedal **6** 41
grandstand, glass-covered ~ **86** 34
granite **99** 42
granular texture **21** 47
grapevine *Sports* **96** 10
graphic art **21**
graphic art studio **21** 27-64
grasp, kinds of ~ **93** 40-46
grasshopper, artificial ~ **58** 68
grass ledge **97** 4
grasstrack racing **87** 24-28
graticule adjuster screw **56** 30
graticule *Hunt.* **56** 31-32
graticule system **56** 31
grave *Church* **12** 23, 34
grave *Script* **23** 31
grave, child's ~ **12** 29
grave, soldier's ~ **12** 32
grave digger **12** 22
grave mound **12** 24
graver **21** 5
graver, round-headed ~ **21** 20
gravestone **12** 26
graveyard **12** 21-41
graveyard chapel **12** 28
graveyard gate **12** 19
graveyard wall **12** 18
gravity fuelling point **64** 32
gravy boat **45** 17
gravy ladle **45** 18
greasepaint stick **112** 46
greasy chalk **21** 26
great hall **10** 30

great organ **7** 1, 43
greave **10** 54
Greek **27** 3
Greek woman **27** 1
green *Ball Games* **90** 82
green bowls **102** 21
green cloth **74** 15
Gretchen style **34** 31
gridiron **113** 4
grid *Theatre* **113** 4
griffin **8** 11
grill *Fair* **105** 33
grinding disc **21** 46
grinding, hollow ~ **99** 22
grinding stone *Ethnol.* **26** 24
grip *Athletics* **95** 45
grip *Films* **110** 21
grip *Rowing* **80** 35
grip *Sports* **102** 57
grip *Winter Sp.* **98** 6
groin vault **16** 31-32; **17** 42
groom *Church* **13** 16
groove *Art* **15** 27
groove *Ball Games* **88** 29
groove *Music. Instr.* **7** 13
groove *Winter Sp.* **98** 39
groschen **59** 13
Grotesque **23** 7
grotto **118** 1
ground, icy ~ **101** 19
ground avalanche **101** 1
ground floor **37** 2
ground game **55** 35
groundsheet ring **75** 26
ground signals **85** 52-54
group **67** 3; **124** 60
grove **26** 5
G sharp minor **1** 60
guard *Fencing* **91** 35, 38, 43
guard, king's ~ **103** 68
guard rail *Roof & Boilerr.* **38** 28
guide rail *Store* **117** 54
guide roller *Films* **109** 29
guiding blade **3** 40
guiding roller **109** 29
guiding slot *Music. Instr.* **3** 41
guilder **59** 19
guillemet **23** 27
guiro **5** 60
guitar **115** 8; **5** 12, 73
guitarist **115** 9
guitar player **115** 9
gulden **59** 19
gules **61** 27
gun, self-cocking ~ **56** 23
gun, self-propelled ~ **62** 57
gun barrel, rifled ~ **56** 34
gun carriage **62** 43
gun carriage, self-propelled ~ **62** 49-74
gun dog **55** 7
gunnel **80** 30
gun slit **55** 52
gun turret **65** 29
gunwale **80** 30
gutter *Dwellings* **37** 6, 11
gutter *Roof & Boilerr.* **38**
guy *Camping* **75** 23
guy line **75** 23
gybe **82** 28

gybing **82** 26
gymkhana **87** 32
gymnastic ball **94** 34
gymnastic club **94** 38
gymnastic hoop **94** 46
gymnastic ribbon **94** 49
gymnastics **94** 33-50
gymnastics apparatus **93** 1-11; **94** 1-6
gymnastics kit **93** 61-63; **94** 51-52
gymnastics, men's ~ **93** 1-11
gymnastics, Olympic ~ **93** 1-11; **94** 1-6
gymnastics, women's ~ **94**
gym shoe **93** 63; **94** 52
gym trousers **93** 62
gypsum *Sculpt. Studio* **20** 29
gypsum powder **20** 29

H

habergeon **10** 51
habit, monk's ~ **12** 55
hair, bobbed ~ **34** 34
hair, closely-cropped ~ **34** 11
hair, curled ~ **34** 33
hair, curly ~ **34** 18
hair, long ~ **34** 1
hair, pinned-up ~ **34** 28
hair, shingled ~ **34** 34
hair, swept-back ~ **34** 28
hair, swept-up ~ **34** 28
hairbrush **28** 7
haircuts **34** 1-25
hair decoration **27** 82
hairdress **26** 9
hairpin *Winter Sp.* **98** 69
hair sieve **67** 66
hairstyles **34** 1-25
hairstyles, girls' ~ **34** 27-38
hairstyles, ladies' ~ **34** 27-38
hairstylist **107** 36; **112** 48
hair trigger **56** 12
half chicken **122** 56
half mask **103** 13
half note **1** 14
half rest **1** 22
half-step **1** 50, 52
half-way line **88** 3
hall **41** 1-29
hall manager **72** 7
hall mirror **41** 6
hall of mirrors **105** 55
Hallstatt period **9** 21-40
halma **73** 26-28
halma board **73** 26
halma man **73** 28
halma piece **73** 28
halter top **31** 64
halyard **60** 2
Hammer and Sickle **60** 21
hammer *Army* **62** 4
hammer *Athletics* **95** 42
hammer *Graphic Art* **21** 14
hammer *Music. Instr.* **3** 35; **6** 3
hammer, iron-headed ~ **20** 16
hammer axe **97** 37
hammer blow **90** 78

jumper *Child. Clothes* **29** 43
jumper *Equest.* **86** 9
jumper, child's ~ **29** 47
jumper, cowl neck ~ **30** 2
jumper, polo neck ~ **30** 7
jumper, short-sleeved ~ **31** 67
jumping **95** 9-41
jumping hoop **104** 58
jumping jack **103** 52
jumping rope **119** 15, 16
jumping saddle **86** 10
jump rope **119** 16
jump-sit-spin **99** 8
jump ski **83** 62
jumpsuit **31** 53
jump throw **89** 3
junk **25** 32
junk stall **105** 60
just **10** 71

K

karabiner **97** 46
karabiner hole **97** 35
karate **96** 18-19
karateka **96** 18
kart **102** 83
karting **102** 82
kayak **80** 4; **25** 12
kayak, folding ~ **80** 61, 62, 67
kayak, one-man ~ **80** 54
kayak, two-seater ~ **80** 61
kayaks **80** 68-70
keel *Rowing* **80** 32
keel *Sailing* **82** 32
keel arch **17** 36
keel, lead ~ **82** 36
keel-centreboard yawl **82** 37-41
keelson **80** 50
keep **10** 4
keep net **58** 28
kegellade chest **7** 12-14
kelson **80** 50
kerb **118** 25
ketchup **45** 43
kettle, brass ~ **42** 14
kettle, whistling ~ **39** 16; **40** 10
kettledrum **4** 57
key *Music. Instr.* **3** 28, 38, 49; **4** 32, 35; **5** 40; **7** 8
key *Town* **124** 4
key, black ~ **6** 5
key, ebony ~ **6** 5
key, iron ~ **9** 32
key, ivory ~ **6** 4
key, white ~ **6** 4
key action **6** 22-39
keyboard instrument **6** 1
keyboard, lower ~ **3** 47
keyboard *Music. Instr.* **3** 28; **5** 40; **6** 4-5
keyboard side **5** 39
keyboard, upper ~ **3** 46
key lever **3** 38, 49; **7** 8
key mechanism **6** 22-39
key rack **123** 3
key signatures **1** 50-54
keys *Music. Not.* **1** 55-68
keystone **17** 23

kicker **89** 10
kicking strap **81** 21
kill *Bullfight. etc.* **116** 30
kill *Hunt.* **55** 38
kimono **25** 40
kindergarten **48**
king **73** 8
King Carnival **103** 58
Kirghiz **25** 22
kit **3** 20
kitchen **39**
kitchen appliances **40**
kitchen chair **39** 43
kitchen clock **39** 20
kitchen cupboard **39** 8
kitchen lamp **39** 39
kitchen roll **40** 1
kitchen scales **106** 84
kitchen table **39** 44
kitchen unit **46** 29
kitchen utensils **40**
kite *Playground* **119** 41, 42
kite, paper ~ **67** 71
kite string **119** 44
knapsack **55** 3
knee-breeches **33** 40
knee cap *Chivalry* **10** 53
kneeler **13** 25
knee lever **6** 45
kneeling front support **92** 20
kneeling position *Free Exerc.* **92** 8
kneeling position *Sports* **102** 28
knee pad *Ball Games* **89** 9
knee pad *Winter Sp.* **100** 17
knee piece **10** 53
knee strap **33** 41
knee swell **6** 45
knife *Swim.* **76** 8
knife *Tablew. etc.* **45** 7, 50
knife, bronze ~ **9** 31
knife, hafted ~ **9** 31
knife rest **45** 11
knife thrower **104** 37
knight *Chivalry* **10** 67
knight *Games* **73** 11
knighting **10** 66
Knight Templar **10** 73
knobkerrie **26** 33
knobkerry **26** 33
knob-leaf capital **14** 14
knockout **96** 40
knot *Ladies' Wear* **31** 47
knot *Underwear etc.* **32** 42
koruna **59** 27
KR-class **81** 63
kris **25** 44
krona **59** 25
krone **59** 24, 26
krummhorn **3** 6
kursaal **120** 8
kymation **15** 19

L

label **54** 4
labret **26** 23
lace, cotton ~ **31** 32
lace **88** 32
lacquered work, incised ~ **18** 6

ladder *Child. Rm.* **47** 5
ladder *Fruit & Veg. Gdn.* **52** 8
ladder *Roof & Boilerr.* **38** 15
ladder, aluminium ~ **50** 35
ladies' wear **30; 31**
ladies' wear department **117** 28
lady *Hist. Cost.* **27** 59, 64, 68, 70, 79
lagging **38** 72
lake dwelling **9** 15
laminate **98** 48
lamp *Dining Rm.* **44** 12
lamp *Nightclub* **115** 26
lamp, fluorescent ~ **49** 32; **117** 23
lamp, pendant ~ **44** 12
lamphouse **106** 44; **109** 39-44
lance *Bullfight. etc.* **116** 17
lance *Chivalry* **10** 81
lance *Ethnol.* **25** 9
lancer **116** 16
lance rest **10** 80
lancet arch **17** 31
lancet window **16** 39-41
land **56** 39
land drill **79** 20
landing area **95** 36, 39
landing *Athletics* **95** 19
landing craft **65** 89, **66** 46
landing flap **64** 38; **85** 29
landing gear housing **63** 15
landing gear hydraulic cylinder **64** 41
landing gear unit, forward-retracting ~ **64** 40
landing gear unit, main ~ **64** 40; **85** 33
landing light **64** 37; **85** 32
landing mat **93** 13; **94** 7
landing net **58** 2
landing pad *Athletics* **95** 36
landing skid **63** 21
landing stage **75** 13; **80** 19
landing unit, main ~ **63** 26
landlord **102** 7, 13
lane arrow **124** 73, 74
lane timekeeper **79** 24
language laboratory **68** 35
languid **7** 28
lansquenet **27** 32
lantern *Art* **16** 45
lantern, Chinese ~ **25** 36
lantern, combined ~ **83** 13
lantern, paper ~ **52** 15; **103** 4
lanyard **81** 19
lapel **33** 5
lapel, silk ~ **33** 8
lap scorer **87** 6
larmier **57** 14
lasso **116** 40; **24** 5
La Tène period **9** 21-40
lattice mast **65** 18
launcher **65** 49
launching container **65** 32
launching housing **66** 26
launching ramp **62** 66
lavatories **114** 31
lavatory **49** 12; **75** 5
lavatory, public ~ **124** 62
lawn **37** 46; **51** 33; **118** 36; **120** 12
lawn rake **51** 3

loudspeaker **42** 10; **71** 12; **108** 46; **114** 15; **115** 12
loudspeaker aperture **106** 19
louis-d'or **59** 5
Louis Seize table **17** 14
lounge *Living Rm.* **42**
lourer **2** 29
louvre shutter **101** 12
low house **102** 76
low relief **20** 33
low tide **77** 7
L-seat **92** 10
L-support **92** 16
ludo **47** 19
luff **81** 42
luffing **82** 9
luge **100** 13
luge, junior ~ **100** 3
luge toboggan **100** 13
luge tobogganer **100** 12
luge toboggan, junior ~ **100** 3
lumber-jacket **30** 38
lumber room door **38** 20
lunge **92** 42
lunging **91** 5
lunging position **91** 5
lunula *Church* **13** 36
lunula *Prehist.* **9** 25
lupin **51** 23
lur **3** 1
lute **5** 1
lute pin **5** 11
lychgate **12** 19
lyre *Music. Instr.* **3** 15

M

machicolation **10** 23
machicoulis **10** 23
machine drum **4** 57
machine gun **62** 32
madeira glass **45** 84
Madonna **11** 51
magazine *Army* **62** 15, 21
magazine *Chivalry* **10** 13
magazine *Flat* **46** 20
magazine *Hunt.* **56** 17
magazine *Police* **71** 25
magazine holder **62** 7
magazine housing **110** 9
magazine repeater **56** 2
magazine rifle **56** 2
magazine spring **56** 18
magic eye **106** 18
magnetic film **108** 21
magnetic film spool **108** 2
magnetic head cluster **109** 28
magnetic head, four-track ~ **109** 51
magnetic head support assembly **108** 3
magnetic sound amplifier **108** 28
magnetic sound deck **108** 20
magnetic sound head **109** 50
magnetic sound recorder **107** 58; **108** 1
magnetic sound recording equipment **107** 58; **108** 1

magnetic sound unit, attachable ~ **109** 50
magnetic sound unit, four-track ~ **109** 50
maharaja **103** 28
mail **10** 62, 63
mainsail **81** 46; **82** 2
mainsheet **81** 28
mains power unit **108** 11
maintained lift **96** 5
majorette **103** 67
major keys **1** 55-68
major second **2** 7
major seventh **2** 12
major sixth **2** 11
major third **2** 8
major triad **2** 1
make-up artist **107** 36; **112** 48
make-up artist, chief ~ **112** 47
make-up gown **112** 44
make-up man, chief ~ **112** 47
make-up table *Theatre* **112** 45
mallet **20** 21
maltese cross mechanism **109** 38
maltese cross movement **109** 38
manager **96** 45
mandarin *Carnival* **103** 29
mandolin **5** 16
manger board **65** 7, 76
manhole cover *Roof & Boilerr.* **38** 46
manhole *Roof & Boilerr.* **38** 45
manikin **19** 31
mannequin **19** 31
manque **72** 22
mantelpiece **123** 24
mantelshelf **123** 24
mantle *Heraldry* **61** 3
mantle clock **42** 16
mantling **61** 3, 14
manual **6** 48; **7** 42, 43, 44, 45
manual, lower ~ **3** 47
manual, upper ~ **3** 46
map **67** 44; **124** 2
maraca **5** 59
marcando **2** 27
marcato **2** 27
marguerite **51** 24
marimbaphone **5** 61
marimba, steel ~ **5** 61
marine sequence **107** 11
mark **82** 17
market woman **105** 65
markiert **2** 27
marking, axillary ~ **57** 74
mark of omission **23** 29
marks, diacritical ~ **23** 30-35
maroon **103** 53
marquise **36** 55
marriage ceremony **13** 14
marshal **10** 75
marten **55** 22
Masai warrior **26** 8
mask *Carnival* **103** 7
mask, clay ~ **67** 75
masked ball **103** 1-48
mask *Films* **110** 4
mask *Sculpt. Studio* **20** 37
mask *Swim.* **76** 10

mask, pressure-equalizing ~ **76** 10
mask, wooden ~ **26** 16
masquerade **103** 1-48, 6-48
massage bath **78** 33
mass book **11** 38
Master **86** 45
Master of foxhounds **86** 45
master volume control **68** 44
mast **81** 4, 11
mat **96** 12
matador **116** 25, 31
matchbox holder **122** 24
mate **73** 15
material *School* **67** 81
material *Store* **117** 59
matinée coat **29** 3
mat sail **25** 33
matte **110** 4
matte box **110** 3
mattress **47** 3; **93** 18
mattress, foam ~ **43** 10
mauerkrone **61** 46
mausoleum **18** 16
Maya temple **24** 20
maypole swing **119** 8
maze **118** 5
meal, complete ~ **122** 17
meal, hot ~ **122** 67
meal of the day **122** 27
meander *Art* **15** 43
measure *Hotel* **123** 60
measure *Music. Not.* **1** 28-42
measure line **1** 42
measuring beaker **123** 60
measuring cylinder *School* **68** 26
measuring tape **117** 38
meat, roast ~ **45** 27
meat chopper **40** 39
meat dish **122** 55
meat plate **45** 26
meat platter **45** 26
mechanism casing **62** 10
medallion **20** 36
Mediaeval **23** 4
medicine cabinet **49** 49
medium **105** 9
medium measure **91** 10
meeting **70** 8
meeting, public ~ **70** 1-15
megaphone **80** 21
melodium **6** 43
melody key **5** 39
melody pipe **3** 10
melody side **5** 39
melody string **3** 30; **5** 24
membership card **72** 14
membrane, parchment ~ **5** 31
membranophones **4** 51-59
memorial chapel **12** 12
memorial plate **12** 14
memorial tablet **12** 14
menagerie **104** 63
menhir **9** 18
menhir group **9** 11
men's wear **33**
men's wear department **117** 12
menu **122** 21
menu card **122** 21
meringue **121** 5

mouthpiece *Music. Instr.* **4** 36; **5** 33, 72
mouthwash **49** 36
move **73** 14
movie audience **109** 5
moviegoer **109** 5
movie house **109** 1
movie projector **109** 24
movie script **107** 45
movie set **107** 7
movie studios **107** 1-13
movie theater **109** 1
movie theater box office **109** 2
movie theater ticket **109** 3
muffler *Sports* **102** 93
muleta **116** 33
mullion *Art* **16** 41
mullion *Dwellings* **37** 35
multiplier reel **58** 59
multirole combat aircraft **63** 8
mummy **24** 21
mural **19** 40
musette **3** 8
musical instrument, automatic ~ **105** 38
musical instruments **3; 4; 5; 6; 7**
musical instruments, popular ~ **5** 1-46
musical notation **1; 2**
music recording studio **107** 14
music recording theatre **107** 14
music rest **7** 36
music stand **7** 36
mustang **24** 4
mute **4** 10; **5** 68
mutule **15** 13
muzzle *Army* **62** 58
muzzle *Game* **57** 45
muzzle *Sports* **102** 71
myrtle **53** 11
Myrtus **53** 11

N

naiad **8** 23
nail, clenched ~ **82** 52
nail, riveted ~ **82** 52
name plate **82** 46
Nansen sledge **100** 18
napkin **45** 9; **122** 47; **123** 48
napkin ring **45** 10
nappy, disposable ~ **28** 22
narcissus **53** 8
nasturtium **53** 4
natural **1** 45, 46, 54
naturist **78** 16
nave **15** 62; **16** 1
navette **36** 55
navigation equipment **85** 13
navigation light *Air Force* **64** 36
navigation light *Airsports* **85** 31
navigation light *Warships* **65** 56
navigation light, side ~ **65** 15
navigation lights **83** 10-14
navy **65**
Neanderthal man **68** 19
neck *Airsports* **85** 70
neck *Game* **57** 3
neck *Music. Instr.* **5** 7, 18

neck *Rowing* **80** 37
neckband **36** 16
neck, cylindrical ~ **9** 40
neckerchief **31** 57
neck flap *Fencing* **91** 14
neck guard *Chivalry* **10** 83
neck guard *Fencing* **91** 14
necklace **36** 2; **9** 25; **24** 14
necklace, coral ~ **36** 34
necklace, cultured pearl ~ **36** 12
necklace, ivory ~ **36** 28
necklace, pearl ~ **36** 32
neck line *Airsports* **85** 71
neckline *Ladies' Wear* **30** 34
neck of violin **4** 2
neck piece **10** 83
neck ring, gold ~ **9** 26
necktie **116** 38
needle head **106** 33
negative flight **85** 9
negligée **27** 66
negress **26** 22
negro **26** 13
negro hut **26** 21
Neolithic period **9** 10-20
neon sign **124** 16
Nereid **8** 23
net *Airsports* **85** 74
net *Ball Games* **90** 13
net *Hunt.* **55** 27
net-cord judge **90** 23
net curtain **42** 35; **44** 14
net post **90** 15
net stocking **103** 10
net strap **90** 14
net vault **17** 45
netting, wire ~ **20** 35
net vendor **85** 74
neume **1** 1
neutral corner **96** 38
new-born baby **28** 5
news, miscellaneous ~ **23** 63
news dealer **124** 75
news in brief **23** 63
news item **23** 50
newspaper **121** 25; **23** 37-70
newspaper heading **23** 39
newspaper holder **121** 26
newspaper page **23** 37
newspaper rack **121** 8
newspaper shelf **69** 16; **121** 8
newsreel camera **110** 26
New Stone Age **9** 10-20
news vendor **124** 75
niche **12** 60
nigger **107** 51
nightclub **115** 1-33
nightdress **32** 16
nightgown **32** 16
nightie **32** 16
nightshirt **32** 37
night spot **115** 1-33
nightwear **32**
nightwear, ladies' ~ **32** 16-21
nightwear, men's ~ **32** 35-37
nine-eight time **1** 39
nine-four time **1** 40
nine men's morris **73** 18, 23-25
nine men's morris board **73** 23
nix **8** 23

nixie **8** 23
nobleman **27** 44
nock **102** 63
noir **72** 21
non-belayer **97** 27
non-printing area **21** 56
Norfolk Island pine **53** 16
nose, false ~ **103** 46
nose rib **84** 36
nose wheel **85** 34
nose wheel, forward-retracting ~ **64** 3
notation, mensural ~ **1** 2
notation, square ~ **1** 1
notch *Army* **62** 22
notch *Hunt.* **56** 66, 70
notch, wedge-shaped ~ **54** 38
note, musical ~ **1** 3-7
notebook **47** 24; **67** 18
note head **1** 3
notes **59** 29-39
notes, medieval ~ **1** 1-2
note stem **1** 4
note tail **1** 4
note values **1** 12-19
novillero **116** 2
nozzle *Household* **50** 67
nuclear reactor casing **66** 67
nude **19** 32
nudist **78** 16
nudist sunbathing area **78** 15
number *Cyc. Racing* **87** 28
number *Equest.* **86** 33, 36
number key *Flea Market* **106** 76
number key *Store* **117** 3
number *Sports* **102** 84
number *Winter Sp.* **98** 37
number one **80** 13
number plate **87** 28; **102** 84
number tab **123** 10
number tag **123** 10
numeral pendants **60** 33-34
numeral pennants **60** 33-34
nun **12** 50
nursery **47**
nursery child **48** 2
nursery education **48** 1-20
nursery teacher **48** 1
nut *Music. Instr.* **4** 13, 20
nutcrackers **45** 49
nymph, artificial ~ **58** 66

O

oak **51** 12
oak tree **51** 12
oar **75** 19; **80** 14, 26, 35-38
oarlock **75** 18; **80** 29, 41
oarsman **80** 12
oasis **26** 4
obelisk **14** 10
Oberwerk **7** 2
obi **25** 41
object ball, red ~ **74** 12
object lens **110** 2
oboe **4** 38
O'Brien technique **95** 50
observation port *Films* **109** 15
obstacle, almost-fixed ~ **86** 8

obstacle, fixed ~ **86** 20
obstruction **88** 51
obverse **59** 8
ocarina **5** 32
Oceanid **8** 23
ocean nymph **8** 23
octave engagement **91** 50
octave, five-line ~ **2** 50
octave, four-line ~ **2** 49
octave, great ~ **2** 44
octave, one-line ~ **2** 46
octave, small ~ **2** 45
octave, three-line ~ **2** 48
octave, two-line ~ **2** 47
odalisque **103** 41
odds **86** 37
offering **11** 60
offertory bag **11** 59
offertory box **11** 55
office building *Films* **107** 4
office *Camping* **75** 1
office *Chivalry* **10** 27
office, manager's ~ **117** 24
offices **107** 4
offside **88** 42
ogee arch **17** 36
oil and vinegar bottle **45** 42
oil burner **38** 58–60
oil gauge *Roof & Boilerr.* **38** 54
oil-heating furnace **38** 57
oil level pipe **38** 53
oil paint **19** 11
oilstone **21** 21
oil tank *Roof & Boilerr.* **38** 44
O-Joller **81** 50
Old Stone Age **9** 1-9
one-design keelboat **81** 62
one-half twist isander **79** 41
one-two **88** 49
on full point **111** 19
on guard line **91** 3
on guard position **91** 18, 33
on/off valve **76** 22
on-the-ground wrestling **96** 8
open gate **98** 65
opening control **110** 8
open vertical gate **98** 67
opera glass **112** 9
opera hat **35** 36
operating handle **106** 81
operating key **68** 45
operator *Theatre* **113** 59
opponent **90** 18
optical sound recorder **107** 60;
  108 6
optical sound recording **108** 9
optical sound recording
  equipment **108** 6
optical sound unit **109** 45
or **61** 24
orangery **118** 3
orchestra *Art* **15** 47
orchestra *Theatre* **112** 25
orchestra pit **112** 24
orchestrion **105** 38; **106** 14
öre **59** 24, 25, 26
organ **7** 1-5, 1-52
organ, automatic ~ **105** 38
organ, portable ~ **3** 56
organ, portative ~ **3** 56

organ, positive ~ **3** 56
organ case **7** 1-5
organ console **7** 36-52
organistrum **3** 25
organ pipes **7** 17-35
ornamental **53** 16
ornamentation, Greek ~ **15** 38-
  43
ornamentation, Romanesque ~
  16 14-16
ornament, Rococo ~ **17** 13
ornaments **2** 14-22
orographic lift **84** 28
Ostiak **25** 17
Ostyak **25** 17
outboard **75** 15; **80** 6, 7
outboard inflatable **83** 1
outboard motor **75** 15; **80** 7; **83** 1,
  21
outboard motorboat **80** 6
outboard speedboat **80** 6
outdrive motorboat **83** 2
outfielder **89** 41
outrigger *Ethnol.* **24** 36
outrigger *Rowing* **80** 42
outrigger canoe **24** 35
outriggers **80** 9-16
outside defender **88** 13
outside forward **88** 16
outside grip **93** 45
outsider **86** 53
oven **39** 13
oven window **39** 14
overall **33** 56
overalls, leather ~ **87** 26
over-and-under shotgun **102** 70
overblouse **31** 61
overblouse, girl's ~ **29** 48
overdress **31** 17
overflow *Bathrm. etc.* **49** 25
overflow *Fish Farm.* **58** 5
overflow *Roof & Boilerr.* **38** 69
overflow basin **118** 23
overflow pipe **38** 69
overgown **27** 36, 50
overgrasp **93** 40
overhead bicycle kick **88** 45
overhead projector **68** 8
overskirt, panniered ~ **27** 83
overtop **29** 48
overtop, knitted ~ **30** 4; **31** 65
owl **59** 2
owl-glass **103** 38
oxer **86** 8
oxeye daisy, white ~ **51** 24
ox hide, painted ~ **26** 11
oxygen tank *Air Force* **64** 2
oyster fork **45** 80

P

pacer **87** 11
pack *Airsports* **85** 44
pack *Hunt.* **55** 33
pack animal **26** 3
pack of hounds **55** 33
pad *Ball Games* **89** 9
pad *Game* **57** 46

pad *Graphic Art* **21** 13
padding, foam rubber ~ **88** 20
paddle boat **77** 12
paddle, double-bladed ~ **80** 39
paddle, double ended ~ **80** 39
paddle *Ethnol.* **25** 14
paddle, single-bladed ~ **80** 34
paddling pool **37** 44; **119** 28
paddock **116** 15
padlock **38** 21
page *Hotel* **123** 18
page, front ~ **23** 38
pageboy **123** 18
pageboy style **34** 35
page heading **23** 52
pagoda, lndian ~ **18** 21
pagoda, multi-storey ~ **18** 1
pail **50** 54
pailoo **18** 3
pailou **18** 3
paint **19** 10
paintbox **48** 6; **19** 10
paintbrush **48** 7; **67** 84
paint container **112** 34
painter *Art. Studio 3* **19** 2
painting **67** 27
painting materials **19** 6-19 .
painting surface **19** 22
painting table **19** 25
painting, watercolour ~ **48** 5
paint room **112** 28-42
paint trolley **112** 36
pair **72** 20
pairing season **55** 9-12
pair skater **99** 4
pajamas **32** 17, 36
palace, Baroque ~ **118** 7
palace, Renaissance ~ **16** 47
palace buildings **14** 29
palace gardens **118** 1-40
Palaeolithic period **9** 1-9
palette **19** 28
palette dipper **19** 29
palette knife **19** 14
paling **52** 10
palisade *Chivalry* **10** 36
palisade *Equest.* **86** 8
palisading **10** 36
palla **27** 10
pallbearer **12** 40
pallet *Music. Instr.* **7** 10
pallette **10** 45
palm **57** 41
palm capital **14** 25
palm column **14** 17
palmette **15** 41
palm rest **62** 13, 19; **102** 45
palm tree **26** 5
pampas grass **51** 8
pamphlet **11** 57
panache **10** 78
Panama hat **35** 16
pan and tilt head **110** 12
Pandean pipes **3** 2
pandora **3** 21
panel, front ~ **32** 24
panel, mirrored ~ **123** 66
panelling, wood ~ **78** 19
panelling, wooden ~ **122** 37
pan *Household* **50** 52

photography, underwater ~ **76** 23

pianino **6** 1

pianissimo **2** 36

pianissimo pianino **2** 37

piano *Music. Instr.* **6** 1, 40

piano *Music. Not.* **2** 35

piano accordion **5** 36

piano action **6** 2-18

piano case **6** 6

pianoforte **6** 1

piano keys **6** 4-5

piano mechanism **6** 2-18

piano pedal **6** 8-9

piano string **6** 7

picador **116** 16

piccolo **4** 30

pick **97** 33

pickpocket **105** 16

picture **43** 20

picture frame **43** 21

picture gate **109** 34

picture house **109** 1

pier *Art* **17** 25

pier, clustered ~ **16** 34

pier, compound ~ **16** 34

pierette **103** 12

pierrot **103** 19

pigeon hole **123** 2

pigmy **26** 41

pigskin **89** 27

pigtail *Hairst. etc.* **34** 6

pigtail wig **34** 5; **27** 77

piked reverse hang **93** 36

pike *Fish Farm.* **58** 17

pike *Free Exerc.* **92** 38

pike, spawning ~ **58** 11

pike pole **116** 17

pilaster **16** 46

pilaster strip **16** 11

pile dwelling **9** 15; **24** 33

pile of arrow **102** 61

pillar *Art* **16** 20

pillar, engaged ~ **16** 35, 46

pillion passenger **124** 36

pillion rider **124** 36

pillow **43** 12-13; **47** 4

pillowcase **43** 12

pillow slip **43** 12

pilot *Music. Instr.* **6** 33

pilot chute **85** 39

pilot flag **60** 23

pilot light **50** 10

pilot light, covered ~ **38** 60

pilot on board **60** 24

pilot tone cable **110** 29

pilot tone generator **110** 30

pilot wire **6** 34

pinafore, bib top ~ **29** 41

pinafore dress **29** 13; **30** 8; **31** 8

pin *Sports* **102** 12

pin, bronze ~ **9** 29

pin, diamond ~ **36** 18

pin, front ~ **102** 1

pin block **5** 22; **6** 18

pinion *Game* **57** 76

pink *Equest.* **86** 13

pinnacle **16** 29

pip **73** 32

pipe *Living Rm.* **42** 12

pipe *Music. Instr.* **3** 57; **7** 16, 29

pipe, cast-iron ~ **37** 14

pipe, vertical ~ *Dwellings* **37** 14

pipe, magic ~ **26** 42

pipe of peace **24** 6

pipe rack *Living Rm.* **42** 11

pipes **7** 17-35

piping **30** 13; **31** 7

pirate *Carnival* **103** 43

pirate *Sailing* **81** 52

pirouette **111** 24

pisciculture **58** 1-19

piste **91** 2

pistol **62** 1

pistol grip *Army* **62** 6, 38

pistol grip *Hunt.* **56** 6

pistol grip *Police* **71** 23

pitcher *Ball Games* **89** 50, 68

pitcher *Prehist.* **9** 35

pitcher's mound **89** 49, 69

pitch number **75** 42

Pithecanthropus erectus **68** 16

piton **97** 38

piton, ringed ~ **97** 39

pitot-static tube **63** 11; **64** 1

pitot tube **63** 11; **64** 1

pivot *Winter Sp.* **99** 6

pix **11** 8; **13** 53

placard **70** 13; **117** 65; **105** 50

place **44** 5; **45** 3-12

place card **45** 13

place mat **44** 4

place setting **44** 5; **45** 3-12

placing judge **79** 25

plaid strap **100** 2

plainclothes policeman **71** 33

plains Indian **24** 3

plainsong notation **1** 1

plait, coiled ~ **34** 38

plaits **34** 30

plaits, coiled ~ **34** 32

planchet **59** 43

plane, two-seater ~ **85** 18

planing boats **83** 38-44

plank cut **21** 4

planking, inner ~ **82** 57

plank, wooden ~ **21** 2

planographic printing method **21** 25-26

plant, anagraceous ~ **53** 3

plant, asclepiadaceous ~ **53** 15

plant, climbing ~ **51** 5; **52** 5

plant, cyperacious ~ **53** 17

plant, ericaceous ~ **53** 12

plant, gesneriaceous ~ **53** 7

plant, indoor ~ **42** 36

plant, liliaceous ~ **53** 13

plant, tiliaceous ~ **53** 9

plants, indoor ~ **53**

plants, propagation of ~ **54**

plaque *Roulette* **72** 12

plaque *Sculpt. Studio* **20** 38

plaster *Art. Studio* **19** 42

plaster cast **20** 4

plaster of Paris **67** 85

Plasticine **48** 12

plate **122** 11

plate armour **10** 65

plate, baby's ~ **28** 28

plate, bottom ~ **45** 3

plate, deep ~ **44** 6; **45** 5

platen *Graphic Art* **21** 31

platen press **21** 29

platform *Art. Studio* **19** 30

play area **118** 44

playback head **108** 25

player **48** 20

player's name **90** 36

playgoer **112** 8

playground, children's ~ **119**

playing card **73** 36

playing card, French ~ **73** 37

play pen **28** 39

playsuit **29** 11, 19, 22

plaza de toros **116** 5

pleasure boat **80** 1

pleat, front ~ **31** 25

plectrum **3** 19; **5** 20

plinth *Art* **15** 31

plinth *Dwellings* **37** 17

plinth, natural stone ~ **37** 85

plough anchor **83** 16

ploughshare **9** 33

plowshare **9** 33

plucking device **3** 19

plume *Chivalry* **10** 78

plume *Heraldry* **61** 36

plumicorn **57** 78

plummet *Fish Farm.* **58** 91

pneume **1** 1

poacher **55** 29

pochette **3** 20

pocket billiards **74** 7

pocket book **71** 36

pocket flap **33** 18

pocket, front ~ **30** 23; **33** 46; **67** 10

pocket, inset ~ **29** 63; **31** 4

point *Game* **57** 10, 31

point *Sculpt. Studio* **20** 15

point, front ~ **97** 49

point guard **97** 50

point-of-aim mark **102** 56

point of arrow **102** 61

point of hook **58** 80

point of release **58** 34

point shoe **111** 30

points of sailing **82** 1-13

poitrel **10** 85

poke bonnet **103** 23; **27** 71

poker **38** 41

polar sledge **100** 18

pole *Athletics* **95** 28

pole *Fish Farm.* **58** 30

pole *Fruit & Veg. Gdn* **52** 28

pole, bamboo ~ **104** 46

pole mast **65** 42; **66** 6

pole vault **95** 28-36

pole vaulter **95** 29

poleyn **10** 53

police **71**

police badge **71** 27

police dog **70** 25; **71** 5, 6

police duties **71** 1-33

police helicopter **71** 1

police identification disc **71** 26

S

squaw **24** 10
stabilizer *Air Force* **63** 22
stabilizer *Sports* **102** 58
stabilizer *Winter Sp.* **98** 49
stabilizer, horizontal ~ **63** 31; **85** 23
stabilizer, vertical ~ **63** 32; **85** 21
stabilizing fin *Air Force* **63** 22
stabilizing fin *Swim* **76** 3
stabilizing layer **98** 49
stabilizing panel **85** 49
stabilizing surface **63** 22
staccato **2** 34
stack *Univ.* **69** 11
staff **1** 43-44
stag call **56** 46
stage *Films* **109** 8
stage *Nightclub* **115** 22
stage *Theatre* **112** 14-27
stage, revolving ~ **113** 31
stage carpenter **113** 45
stage curtain **109** 10
stage designer **112** 37
stage director **113** 30
stagehand **112** 28; **113** 46
stagehouse **113** 1-60
stage light **113** 14
stage lighting **115** 23
stage lighting unit **113** 14
stage manager **113** 30
stage rehearsal **112** 21-27
stag, rutting ~ **55** 12; **57** 4
staghound **86** 47
stag jump **92** 40; **99** 7
stag leap **92** 40; **99** 7
staircase **37** 72
staircase, outside ~ **14** 33
staircase window **37** 81
stair light **41** 22
stake *Roulette* **72** 13
stake net **58** 94
stalactite vault **18** 17
stalking **55** 1-8
stalls, front ~ **112** 19
stall turn **85** 4
stamp, impressed ~ **59** 35
standard lamp **46** 37
standard of the German Federal President **60** 14
stand *Bullfight etc.* **116** 8
stand *Circus* **104** 57
stand, hydraulic ~ **107** 50
stand, raised ~ **55** 14, 14-17
standing-in position **94** 16
standing position **102** 27
standing stone **9** 18
standing take-off pike dive **79** 40
standing wrestling **96** 6
stapelia **53** 15
star *Films* **107** 27, 28
star *Sailing* **81** 55
Stars and Stripes **60** 18
Star-Spangled Banner **60** 18
start *Athletics* **95** 1-6, 3
starter **79** 30
starter's flag **119** 34
starting and finishing buoy **82** 14
starting block *Athletics* **95** 1
start *Motorboats etc.* **83** 28, 29
starting block *Swim.* **79** 27

starting dive **79** 29
starting line **83** 30
starting place **79** 27
starting position **92** 1
starting price **86** 37
star wheel *Graphic Art* **21** 39
stateof play **90** 38
stationary rings **93** 4
station of the Cross **11** 54
station preset button **106** 20
station selector button **106** 20
statue **118** 10; **15** 5; **20** 32
statue, stone ~ **118** 2
statuette, ivory ~ **9** 8
stave *Music. Not.* **1** 43-44
stayer **87** 14
stay rope **96** 37
stay-warm plate **28** 28
stay wire **93** 10; **94** 5; **96** 37
steam **50** 11
steam hole **50** 14
steaming light **65** 55
steam radio **106** 16
steam slit **50** 14
steam turbine generator **66** 58
steeple **12** 2
steeplechase *Athletics* **95** 7-8
steeplechase *Equest.* **86** 20-22
steering line *Airsports* **85** 41
steering line *Rowing* **80** 52
steering rudder **80** 51-53
steering runner **99** 45
steering wheel **102** 89
steersman *Winter Sp.* **100** 20
stein **106** 53
Steinheim man **68** 17
stela **11** 43; **15** 33
stele **11** 43; **15** 33
stem *Ship* **65** 3
stem, straight ~ **82** 40
stem, wire ~ **6** 29
stem cutting **54** 25
stenography **23** 13
step *Hall* **41** 24
step *Mountain* **97** 17
step *Roof & Boilerr.* **38** 27
step *Swim* **32**, 37
step-cut, hexagonal ~ **36** 62
step-cut, octagonal ~ **36** 52
step-cut, rectangular ~ **36** 50
step-cut, rhombus ~ **36** 59
step-cut, round hexagonal ~ **36** 64
step-cut, square ~ **36** 51
step-cut, trapezium ~ **36** 57
step-cut, triangular ~ **36** 60-61
stepladder **50** 35
stepping stones **37** 45
steps *Circus* **104** 20
steps *Dwellings* **37** 39
steps *Household* **50** 35
steps, front ~ **37** 66
steps, wooden ~ **38** 25
stereobate **15** 4
stereo effect **107** 30
stereo equipment **42** 9; **114** 22-23
stereo sound **108** 35
stereo system **42** 9; **114** 22-23

stern **65** 26; **82** 29
stern light **65** 62
stern light, white ~ **83** 14
stern ramp **65** 91
stern, square ~ **82** 43
stetson hat **116** 37
steward *Cyc. Racing* **87** 4
steward *Election* **70** 10
stick **3** 35; **4** 14, 56
stick blade **99** 32
sticker *Music Instr.* **6** 30; **7** 9
stick, forked ~ **54** 13
stick handle **99** 31
sticking paper **67** 50-52
stile *Household* **50** 36
stile *Roof & Boilerr.* **38** 16
stiletto beard **34** 13
stillhunting **55** 1-8
still life group **19** 27
stilts **105** 49
stitching, decorative ~ **31** 5
stock *Hunt.* **56** 3, 4, 6, 13
stock *Plant Propagn.* **54** 33
stocking **115** 32
stocking, knee-high ~ **32** 9
stola **27** 9
stole, fur ~ **115** 30
Stone Age idol **9** 8
stoneblock **20** 5
stonecrop **51** 7
stone lithography **21** 25-26
stone *Sculpt. Studio* **20** 5
stone *Swim.* **78** 22
stones, faceted ~ **36** 42-71
stool **67** 58
stop *Music. Instr.* **6** 44; **7** 6
stop knob *Music. Instr.* **6** 44; **7** 6
stop lever **5** 42
stop line **124** 50
stopper *Music. Instr.* **7** 35
stops **23** 16-29
stop tab **7** 39
storage box *Child Rm.* **47** 2
storage door **39** 6
storehouse **10** 13
storey roof **18** 2
storm front **84** 24
storm-front soaring **84** 23
storm lantern **75** 29
storm signal **77** 4
stove, cylindrical ~ **106** 4
stove, tiled ~ **122** 34
stove bench **122** 36
stove door **106** 7
stovepipe **106** 5
stovepipe elbow **106** 6
stove screen **106** 8
stove tile **122** 35
straddle **95** 23
straddle jump **95** 23
straddle position **93** 30
straddle seat **92** 18
straight ball **102** 17
straight hang **93** 38
straight header **79** 12
straight inverted hang **93** 37
straight thrust **91** 7
strake, outside ~ **82** 50
strampler **29** 23
strap *Cyc. Racing* **87** 22

MORE OXFORD PAPERBACKS

Details of a selection of other books follow. A complete list of Oxford Paperbacks, including The World's Classics, Twentieth-Century Classics, OPUS, Past Masters, Oxford Authors, Oxford Shakespeare, and Oxford Paperback Reference, is available in the UK from the General Publicity Department, Oxford University Press (JH), Walton Street, Oxford OX2 6DP.

In the USA, complete lists are available from the Paperbacks Marketing Manager, Oxford University Press, 200 Madison Avenue, New York, NY 10016.

Oxford Paperbacks are available from all good bookshops. In case of difficulty, customers in the UK can order direct from Oxford University Press Bookshop, 116 High Street, Oxford, Freepost, OX1 4BR, enclosing full payment. Please add 10 per cent of published price for postage and packing.

ENGLISH ART 1870–1940

Dennis Farr

Dennis Farr traces English art from Whistler to Ben Nicholson and Henry Moore. A central theme is the breakdown of the old academic tradition and the increasing importance of those innovators who worked outside the established art societies. This was the period of English Impressionism, Art Nouveau, the Arts and Crafts Movement, the Bloomsbury Group, and Art Deco, and the architectural 'free style'.

For this paperback edition the author has revised the text and updated the bibliography.

'a major contribution to the study of modern painting, sculpture, architecture, and design in this country . . . as comprehensive as one is ever likely to get' *Museums Journal*

'a succinct, personal and extremely readable narrative' *New Statesman*

'His book will command wide professional respect and yet equally delight the non-specialist public.' *British Book News*

VISION AND DESIGN

Roger Fry

Roger Fry's trenchant rejection of nineteenth-century Academicians was part of his attempt to open the eyes of a whole generation to the special formal properties of art. The range of his interests was enormous: the twenty-five essays included in this collection cover topics from Negro art to Giotto and from William Blake to contemporary domestic architecture. Among the central themes explored by Fry are the relationships between ancient and modern art, and between art and life.

A SHORT HISTORY OF THE MOVIES
Gerald Mast

This classic account of the history of film contains material on the 'Neue Kino' of West Germany, political films of the Third World, the American new wave of the seventies, and much more of interest to film buffs.

'This is the kind of literate, non-ideological book that should be used in schools' *Observer*

'The *Short History* is fun to flip through and an excellent reference book; it has an acute appendix, and many illustrations' *Times Educational Supplement*

ARTHUR SULLIVAN
A Victorian Musician
Arthur Jacobs

Arthur Jacobs has seized on new documentary evidence, which includes revelations of Sullivan's sexual adventures, to paint a fascinating portrait of W. S. Gilbert's famous partner—the man, his music, and the Victorian musical world which he came to dominate.

'a wealth of anecdote, insight and incidental material . . . make the book fascinating reading as well as indispensable scholarship' *Classical Music Weekly*

AN ABC OF MUSIC

Imogen Holst

Foreword by Benjamin Britten

An introduction to the language of music, a dictionary of musical terms, a brief history of music, a guide to harmony and form: this brilliantly lucid book is all these, and more. It can be read by absolute beginners—no knowledge is assumed. But anyone, however musical, will find it useful, stimulating, and packed with information.

Oxford Paperback Reference

THE CONCISE OXFORD COMPANION TO THE THEATRE

Edited by Phyllis Hartnoll

The Concise Oxford Companion to the Theatre is an essential handbook for the theatre-goer or the drama student. It contains entries on actors and actresses from Sarah Bernhardt to Alec McCowen; on theatrical companies and theatre buildings from the Abbey Theatre in Dublin to the Yvonne Arnaud Theatre in Guildford; and on dramatists from Sophocles to Samuel Beckett. The range of the volume is international, and also includes explanations of technical terms, and notes on practical and historical aspects of stagecraft and design.

For this concise version, based on Phyllis Hartnoll's third edition of *The Oxford Companion to the Theatre,* each article has been considered afresh, and most have been recast and rewritten, often with the addition of new material.

THE CONCISE OXFORD HISTORY OF BALLET

Horst Koegler

This is the most comprehensive one-volume reference book on ballet in the English language. There are over five thousand entries on every aspect of ballet over the past four hundred years: ballets themselves, choreographers, composers, designers, theatres, ballet schools, companies, dancers, and technical terms.

The author, Horst Koegler, is a well-known German ballet critic, and his dictionary is an indispensable work of reference for anyone who is interested in ballet, whether as a professional, amateur, or spectator.

THE CONCISE OXFORD DICTIONARY OF MUSIC

Third Edition

Michael Kennedy

The third edition of this famous music dictionary has been thoroughly updated and revised. Biographies and technical terms alike—nearly everything has been written afresh. There is a vastly increased coverage of early music, and of music and musicians of the twentieth century. The articles on major composers now include comprehensive lists of works. As a result, this will prove the indispensable compact music dictionary for the 1980s.

THE CONCISE OXFORD DICTIONARY OF OPERA

Second Edition

Harold Rosenthal and John Warrack

Since its first publication *The Concise Oxford Dictionary of Opera* has established itself as an invaluable source of information on all aspects of opera. It contains entries on individual operas, composers, librettists, singers, conductors, technical terms, and other general subjects connected with opera and its history. This enlarged second edition includes many new articles on composers and performers, details of casts at first performances, and much additional information on the development of opera in different countries. Many of the existing entries have been rewritten and updated.

'You will ... discover here an enormous amount of information not available elsewhere.' *Daily Telegraph*

Oxford Paperback Reference

THE OXFORD COMPANION TO THE DECORATIVE ARTS

Edited by Harold Osborne

The Oxford Companion to the Decorative Arts is an authoritative guide to those arts whose products, although made for a purpose, are chiefly valued for their craftsmanship and the beauty of their appearance.

Under the editorship of Harold Osborne, who also edited *The Oxford Companion to Art,* expert contributors provide introductions to all the main fields of craftsmanship. This invaluable handbook includes entries not only on important craftsmen and schools throughout the world, but also on particular cultures and periods. A celebration of the pride and skills of generations of craftsmen.

The text is illustrated throughout with photographs and line-drawings, and there is a selective bibliography of nearly 1,000 titles.

'Admirable as a reference book, but guaranteed to encourage leisurely browsing.' *Yorkshire Post*

Oxford Paperback Reference

THE OXFORD ILLUSTRATED HISTORY OF BRITAIN

Kenneth O. Morgan

Now in a lavishly illustrated large-format paperback with 24 colour plates. 150,000 copies of the hardback have been sold.

'Without doubt, this will serve as the standard one-volume history of Britain for the rest of the century.' *Sunday Times*

'the best buy of the year in historical publishing. It belongs in every school satchel, on every student's desk, in every library's catalogue . . . on everyone's coffee table . . . wherever readers have a real curiosity to discover, in words and pictures, the current stage of historical inquiry in the field of British history, from the Romans to Thatcher.' *History Today*

'lavishly illustrated in a way that both embellishes the volume and illuminates the text.' *British Book News*

'a lively and stimulating overview by a selection of our best younger historians, scholarly but very readable.' *Observer*

THE CONCISE OXFORD HISTORY OF MUSIC

Gerald Abraham

The Concise Oxford History of Music provides an account of the history of music as scholarly, as up to date, and as complete as is possible within the confines of a single volume. Gerald Abraham, one of the most highly respected contemporary writers on music, shares his knowledge of composers and compositions and his insight into the historical development of styles. The judgements are penetrating and the richness of content demands—and rewards—continuous attention.

Dr Abraham covers the whole history of music from its first recorded emergence in early civilizations to the death of Stravinsky. He also discusses non-Western music. He provides numerous music examples and the book is illustrated with plates throughout.

'provides all the answers clearly, sharply, authoritatively . . . the wonder here is that one man in his listening and researching can cover so much ground and illuminate it' Edward Greenfield, *Guardian*

THE OXFORD–DUDEN PICTORIAL ENGLISH DICTIONARY

Business and Technical

Certain kinds of information are better conveyed visually than by written definitions. *The Oxford–Duden Pictorial English Dictionaries* offer more than an ordinary illustrated dictionary; they present the vocabulary of a particular subject alongside a picture illustrating it. An alphabetical index is also provided for easy cross-reference.

This volume describes objects used or referred to in business—from the supermarket to the Stock Exchange—and in industry, transport, and communications.

Oxford Paperback Reference

THE OXFORD–DUDEN PICTORIAL ENGLISH DICTIONARY:

Science and Medicine

Certain kinds of information are better conveyed visually than by written definitions. This dictionary offers more than an ordinary illustrated dictionary; it presents the vocabulary of a particular subject alongside a picture illustrating it. An alphabetical index is also provided for easy cross-reference.

This vocabulary of Astronomy, Geography, Dentistry, Mathematics, Natural History, and much more is given in this dictionary.

Oxford Paperback Reference